D1066873

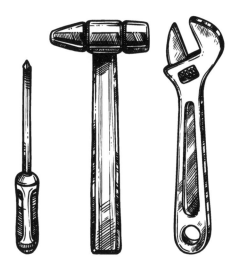

THE

PASTOR'S TOOLBOX

A Practical Guide to a Pastor's Tasks

Dr. Rod Nielsen

Cover design: Jason Sell

Cover Images: Chepko, istockphoto.com, 2015.

Interior design: Jason Sell

Interior Images: Seamartini, depositphotos.com, 2017.

ISBN 979-8-9859111-1-4

Dedicated to Agape Christian Church of La Porte, Indiana,
where I learned how to do the work of a pastor, and to the Associate
Ministers, interns, and men and women I mentored,
for whom I developed this material.

Contents

Forward

Christian Churches need pastors. Christian colleges and seminaries train men and women to serve as lead pastors, preaching pastors, music pastors, outreach pastors, spiritual development pastors, and many other variations of pastoral roles. Some men and women are able to specialize in one of these roles. Many, especially in small churches must fill several or all of the different roles.

In college and seminary aspiring pastors are taught Bible, theology, world view, and philosophy. They are taught homiletics and pastoral counseling. They are even taught church growth techniques. Noticeably missing is teaching the fundamental day to day tasks of ministry: the steps of officiating a funeral or wedding; the work of preparing to preach while balancing other responsibilities; what to take in account when counseling church members; what it takes to lead meaningful worship; and other practical considerations of the work of being a pastor.

Many large churches recruit and train pastoral staff from within their own or another congregation. Some colleges and seminaries offer classes in Bible and theology in a local church where men and women can be trained without relocating to a college or seminary campus. Where will these pastors in training find the practical information needed to do the work congregations expect a pastor to know how to do?

Small churches, of which there are thousands, often hire beginning pastors. If these men and women have not been taught they will have to learn as they go. The Pastor's Toolbox is like the YouTube videos that teach how to use the tools we own to their best application. We buy tools (or receive them as gifts) but actually using them takes time to learn. It is my prayer that The Pastor's Toolbox will help you learn how to do the tasks expected of you as a pastor.

This book was written to help men and women starting out in pastoral ministry. The many example messages, outlines, and premarital counseling ideas will give new pastors a boost. Helpful ideas for the various situations they will be required to attend will also serve those who have been pastoring for a season. Veteran pastors who are training interns or mentoring unseasoned or rookie pastors will find a workable teaching outline.

Acknowledgments

First and foremost I offer my greatest "Thank You" to my Savior Jesus Christ who changed a shy naïve young man into a preacher and pastor. Finding a job as a pastor is not really difficult. Learning how to be a pastor requires the grace of a patient God.

Secondly I thank my bride, Lisa Nielsen, who walked every step of the way beside me, before me, and behind me in my forty years being a pastor. Her many sacrifices being a pastor's wife made possible my opportunity to serve in this capacity. Her wisdom guided me more often and in more ways than I could every count. Her love gave me the strength to endure the difficult times and enhanced the joy of the great times. Her skill in editing and clarifying the content of this teaching made it possible.

I thank the membership of Agape Christian Church of La Porte, Indiana, who supported me and learned from me. Their love for Christ and for me motivated me to be the best pastor and preacher I could be. The men and women who served and worked alongside me in the ministry of our church are forever in my thoughts and prayers.

Finally I thank my brothers Dale Nielsen and Andy Nielsen who assisted in editing, and Dr. Don Green, Dr. Gary Johnson, Dr. Tommy Oaks, Ben Crostreet, Patrick Pence, and Carter Perry, who reviewed an early manuscript, offered suggestions, and encouraged me to publish.

Introduction

You just graduated from a Christian college or seminary and are in your first preaching ministry. You are excited to share some of what you learned and your understanding of the Bible. You did well in homiletics and exegetical studies so you are ready to take the pulpit by storm. You are prepared to lead Bible studies and Sunday school. This is going to be a great ministry. Your church is going to grow like corn in Indiana!

The first year is speeding by. You have already learned how to balance your study time with other church responsibilities. You have good leaders around you, elders and deacons, and other volunteers. All is well in your world.

One afternoon you get a call from a local funeral home. Someone has died and the family requests that you officiate a funeral for their loved one. Then it hits you, "I've never done a funeral. I don't know how to do a funeral! What do I do? What do I say? When will I find time to prepare a funeral and still get my sermon and Bible study prepared?"

At this point you realize you will have to just do the best you can. Your sermon may be a little short this week and Bible study will be a healthy discussion. You scramble for some sort of funeral manual. Finding one you think, "There must be a sample funeral and funeral message in here somewhere. Why didn't they teach me how to do this in seminary?" And then you think, "What other things have I not been taught?"

Christian colleges and seminaries are doing the best they can to teach students how to prepare and preach sermons, how to study the Bible and teach it accurately, and how to lead a church using modern church growth methods. There just isn't room in the curriculum for teaching how to conduct a funeral or wedding, however your congregation expects you to know how to do it. Thus begins your personal journey to rise to this challenge. Allow me to join you on your journey.

In my thirty–nine plus years of ministry, with one congregation, I had to learn for myself how to do these and many other practical things in ministry. My first funeral was for the patriarch of our small church and I was unprepared for it. I read some appropriate scripture and added a poem and a couple of prayers. The family was grateful that I tried but I knew I had failed them. I did my best but it was woefully inadequate in providing comfort to the family. I want to help you avoid that experience.

I am retired from full–time ministry now but continue my love affair with teaching young or new pastors how to do the job of ministry. This book is a toolbox of practical tips on how to do the tasks of ministry for which there often is no class in seminary or Christian college. I will discuss how to lead a funeral or wedding, the job (not the art) of preaching, some considerations for pastoral counseling, pastoral visitation, your role in the local community, plus some thoughts on leading worship.

The issues discussed are the things I taught interns and other ministers I have mentored. These are the practical tasks that your congregation expects you to know how to do. This is a "How To" book.

Let me say from the start, whatever you do as a pastor, do the hard work to serve well, as unto the Lord. Never try to get by on your wit and charm. The people you serve deserve your absolute best effort. Professor Dr. Jeff Gill at Grace Theological Seminary shared this thought from pastor and author Leith Anderson, God's people have a right to competent leadership, even when we're feeling tired, angry, frustrated, or lonely.

Please understand, like any position in your working life there will be people who discourage you, blame you, and criticize you.

They will say things such as, "Your preaching is not as good as the well–known radio preacher", "The guy at First Church is a better worship leader," or "A different counselor I have been seeing has helped me more than you." Families will leave your church for a different one that offers other resources and programs, or they will leave because the children want to go where their friends go. Some will leave because they have a conflict with another church member.

You cannot control other people. Do not get discouraged. Learn from the ones who truly want to help you grow. Hear the rest but do not dwell on them. As long as you know that you have given it your best, trust that, as Acts 2:47 tells us, it is God who adds to the church.

Dr. Rod Nielsen

Chapter One
Help! I've Never Done a Funeral

When a family's loved one dies they almost always expect some sort of funeral to go with burial or cremation. Interestingly, even people who are not Christ believers usually will request a pastor to lead the funeral. Leading a funeral is not part of your job. It is part of your ministry. What I mean is that you serve the family with the same love and dedication that you demonstrate in other areas of ministry. While some parts of your role as a pastor of a church are just tasks that need to be done (i.e. the business of the church), leading a funeral is a time for you to serve a family, bring them comfort, and help them experience closure.

A well–led funeral service will be greatly appreciated. I have officiated close to 200 funerals in my ministry. It took a little while but I learned to do them in a personal way that truly brought comfort to the grieved. One woman in our town, who had attended several funerals I led, came to me before the funeral of a prominent member of our community and said, "I'm glad you're doing this. You're my favorite funeral doer!"

Your efforts to connect with the family in a personal way is what brings comfort. They want to know that you understand and empathize with their grief. You may have done other funerals, but this is the one that matters to them. How you serve that family right now is very important, however, the best things you do for the family who has lost a loved one is what you did for that loved one while he was living.

When you are new to town get to know the funeral directors. If you have not already done that, do it now. Discover if there are certain cultural norms for that community that will be expected from you. Funeral directors are your partners. Learn the things the funeral home will be doing and how they will affect what you do. You will want to know what facilities and comforts they provide. Find out what kind of dais, pulpit or lectern, and microphone they use. Learn what equipment they have for playing music and videos. Purchase a good well–fitting suit with shirt, shoes, and ties that present a professional appearance. Let's consider some important aspects about your role in conducting a funeral.

The Beginning

The process begins immediately upon being informed of a death and funeral. Start thinking about how you will be personal with the family. You may have been at the bedside with them when death occurred or you may have been on a lake fishing. Immediately think of the family members as individuals who are experiencing grief that a short time ago was not on their minds.

As you spend time comforting them, understand that there is no right or wrong way to grieve. Everyone is different and must find his or her own way through the grieving process. Assure them of this fact. When talking with them, asking questions can help them express their feelings. Ask about their relationship with the deceased. Ask about the changes they expect going forward. Ask about what they need to do in the coming weeks. When they can verbalize their feelings, they can better control their expressions of grief.

There is also no right time or length of grieving. Some people will struggle with grief for months or even years. Let the family mourn. Allow them to cry. Tears can be quite cathartic. When a loved one dies grief is the cost of loving. Your role is not to make sense of this death. Your role is to provide comfort however long they need you, and it all begins right now.

Do not make this event about you. Even if you have been there yourself and know exactly how they feel, do not say it. This is not about you. It is about them. Tell them you understand, show sympathy, cry with them, show your love, and remind them of God's love. Do not tell them this death was "God's will," especially if it is a child. It is never God's will for anyone to die. Death is the result of sin in the world. God's will is life. Speak with them about how God grieves when people die and how He sent His Son to die for our sins so that we can enjoy eternal life. Do not be preachy, just love them with God's love.

Meeting with the family

For the sake of personalization, let's walk through the funeral of "Chuck". Gather with the family to plan the funeral as soon as is convenient for them and you. You have to fit this into your busy schedule so do not waste time. Ask every one of the family to join in if they wish to be part of planning. If possible have this visit at one of their homes. Take a notebook and pen with you and tell them you will be taking notes that will help you prepare to honor Chuck. Your purpose at this meeting is threefold: to determine how the family members are handling the death, to get to know Chuck (even if you are already well known to each other), and to develop an idea of what the service will look like.

Listen to them. Pay attention to their concerns, fears, and hurt. Ask questions about Chuck and let them talk. Encourage them to tell stories, share anecdotes and remembrances. They will show you pictures. Look at them closely getting to know him. Listen for "pet names" or nicknames. Learn how to pronounce his name. In your message use the name by which they know him. If they call him Chuck do not call him Charles.

Even if you know Chuck personally, approach this as if you do not know him at all. Ask them to introduce him to you as if you had never met. Take copious notes because this will help you write a message for the funeral. Many families think of the funeral as a "Celebration of Life" so you will want to talk about his life. You want to know him well enough to talk about him in a personal way. Before this meeting is complete ask the family, *"What is the main thing you would like your guests to think about your father? If someone who does not know him but is attending out of respect for you, what would you want them to learn about him?"* You should be able to glean at least one specific thought that describes him. Do not be surprised if you hear many of the same things every time. *"He loved his family. He was a hard-working man. He had a good sense of humor."* Take note of these thoughts, but listen carefully for that one unique nugget. The family will appreciate how you brought everything together to honor their loved one.

Unless you know Chuck is a Christian do not assure the family that he is in Heaven with Jesus, and do not say it in your message. Be as positive as you can with reassurance of God's love for all men, but you undermine the Gospel if you declare that a non–believer is in Heaven. Neither should you say that he missed out on eternal life. The family may be thinking it, but it is not for you to say.

In this meeting you will not necessarily plan the funeral but you will begin the process. Ask them about any scriptures that were meaningful to him. Ask about favorite songs that could be used in the service. Ask about any family members who may wish to partic-ipate with a song, a story, or a reading.

You must realize that some families will give you next to nothing to work with. This is when you must really meet the challenge.

Preparing your Message

The family is depending on you to give them a message of comfort. Be sure your message is about Chuck. Some funerals I have attended were so generic it was clear the pastor knew very little, if anything, about the one he was burying. Do not create one funeral that you will use every time by simply changing the name. Make this funeral as personal as you can even if you use some ideas repeatedly. This funeral is about this man, not someone you buried last year.

Hopefully you were able to get to know him through the family during your visits as they told you stories and shared remembrances. From these you should be able to talk about Chuck in a personal way. Do not insert yourself into the stories unless they were truly your experiences with him.

Weave the things you have learned about him into a smooth narrative. Do not simply read a list of events and happenings or things he did. Imagine you are telling stories around the kitchen table. If possible stay away from negatives. The family already knows them and do not need or want to think about that right now. Try to verify the stories. Some family members may not agree with what the others told you. You do not want someone in attendance hearing you and thinking that what you are saying is not true. I once led a funeral for a friend's wife. He shared about their loving relationship. The day before the service, another family member came to my office to tell me that the family all hated him because he treated their sister so poorly. You cannot always know for sure but do your best to speak truthfully.

In your message you will probably be doing some kind of eulogy. A eulogy is not simply reading the obituary from the newspaper. A eulogy is a speech or writing in praise of a person, especially an oration in honor of a deceased person. You want to speak of good things or fun things the family can think about. It is okay to make them laugh, but do not be a jokester. Help them remember how much they love him and he loved them, and what he brought to the family dynamic. Celebrate his life as much as you can.

There is no right length for a funeral message. I suggest you do not let it be too lengthy. Most people are not interested in listening to you for very long. Say enough to create a good feeling about their loved one but not long enough to be boring. The late Dr. James Strauss, long–time professor at Lincoln Christian Seminary, used to say, *"It is a sin to be boring when preaching."* It is even more so at a funeral.

I believe you should include the Gospel in your message even if the deceased or family are not Christians. You do not have to preach an evangelistic message and you certainly do not want to lead an altar call. Simply remind believers of Jesus' love and sacrifice, and introduce the idea to non–believers. Studies have shown that this is a time when most people are as open to the Gospel as they will ever be. You can invite them to meet with you if they are interested in learning more.

Before the funeral, practice your message. Practice out loud. Make sure you are comfortable speaking the words you have written. Prepare well. Do not try to "wing it" even if you are good on your feet. The family deserves a well–prepared funeral.

You may have a basic funeral outline that you use often as long as you still make it personal to this specific individual and this family. Some ideas simply work. When you find something that works such as a basic message or a catchy illustration, keep it and use it.[1] I advise you to not use a particular idea or illustration just to use it. It must truly fit the context.

You will need to be prepared for all kinds of funerals. You will eventually do funerals for church members, non–church members,

---

1   Appendix A includes several illustrations I have used that always work well.

individuals well known in the community, paupers, very important persons, suicides, murder victims, accident victims, babies, young people, old people, people you know well and some you do not know at all. Think about how they are different and how you can approach the funeral accordingly.[2]

When the funeral is over keep a copy of what you said and did along with a copy of the obituary. You are likely to have more than one funeral for a specific family. If you served them well they will probably call on you the next time they lose someone so it is helpful to remember how you did the last one. You would not want to use the exact funeral you used for a previous family member. Also, keep orderly records of every funeral you lead. This will be more valuable than you may think right now. If record keeping is not your strength, keep records anyway. That is what file cabinets are for.

Preparing the Funeral Service

There is no "correct" way to do a funeral service. You do not have to be as creative as if you were producing a play, but you should not simply use one form just filling in the blanks with new names. Make each funeral personal to the deceased and family.

Prepare a copy of the service for the funeral director. It will help him or her to know when to start music, turn on microphones, and begin dismissal. Trust the funeral director, yet without being confrontational, take charge of the funeral itself.

Working with the family, create an order of service. Who will speak and when? Who will sing a song or read a poem or tribute? What military or other honors will be done and how? Some families are happy to ask guests to share a thought if they desire. With the family's permission, at some time in the service invite people to share a short thought. This can be risky because some people, once they start talking can't stop. Be prepared for this. Then thank each one who shared.

---

2   Appendix B offers examples of funerals for specific situations.

Everyone participating in the service should be discouraged from trying to do it extemporaneously. Even one who was marvelous in debate club will often find it much more difficult to speak at a funeral. Also, remind them to have a back–up plan if they intend to use electronic technology. Sometimes the notes on their cell phone just will not show up.

If someone is going to sing a song, talk to the singer about what she or he will sing. Encourage him or her to practice well. Reinforce that, *"This is honoring your loved one. It is not about you."* Help the singer prepare in order to get through it without falling into weeping. Place songs or readings in the order of service before things get too emotional. Give them at least an outline of the service so they will know when they are up.

Those who are going to read a poem or tribute should be encouraged to prepare as well. They too need to remember that this is about the loved one. Typed words are much easier to read under stress than handwritten notes. I strongly encourage those who will participate to prepare their thoughts on computer or word processor. If they get too emotional to finish reading, you can take over and read their words for them if they are typed. Suggest that they use large enough font so that they can read it even as their eyes fill with tears. Finally, reiterate that they should practice reading aloud. It is possible to write things that one's tongue cannot say. They can identify difficult words or phrases when practicing.

Visitation

It is not necessary for you to attend the entire visitation. I encourage you to arrive at the funeral home when the family comes for private time before visitation begins. Pay attention to how they are handling their emotions. Respond if you think it is necessary. Remind them that they will be very busy for the next few hours. Assure them that if they are tired no one will be upset with them if they go to a private place (every funeral home has one for them) to rest. If they get tired of being on their feet they may sit down and let guests come to them.

The Funeral

You should arrive at the funeral home early enough to make necessary changes or take care of any problems that may have arisen. Check on the family, offering comfort or encouragement. Meet with the funeral director. Make sure all songs and videos to be played are ready. Go over any changes that have been made to the elements or order of the funeral. Check on anyone who is participating in the service to be sure they are prepared and ready.

Sometime before the service is to begin find a quiet place to go over your notes or manuscript. You may find that you have doubts as to whether your message will provide the comfort you seek for the family. You have prayerfully prepared. Now trust that God, through His Holy Spirit, has guided your pen and your thoughts. Lead the funeral service with confidence. I have also found it beneficial to go to a private place with the funeral director to pray for the service.

When the service is over the funeral home staff will release the guests to file past the coffin and pay last respects. I encourage you to stand nearby. Some people will want to thank you. Some will want to hug you. Some will want a copy of your message. Bring two extra copies of the funeral service. Leave one with the family and have another to give to that one guy who asks.

I usually stay in the room when the coffin is closed. I feel like I represent the family in doing so as the family is usually asked to retire to their cars before the closing.

The Committal

The committal is what you say at the gravesite as you commit the body to the grave if that is part of the plan. This is your final word about and for the deceased. You will often ride to the cemetery with the funeral director in the lead car. When you arrive at the gravesite you will wait for the family and others to gather at the hearse. The pall bearers will be guided by the funeral home staff and you will lead the procession to the grave.

Once everyone is assembled you will share your final thoughts. You should not simply repeat what you said in the funeral service. This is the final "Good-bye". Keep it short. If the deceased is a Christian remind them that he or she no longer lives in this body. For one who is not a believer, remind them that the grief they feel is the price of love. If they didn't love, they wouldn't grieve.

Prepare this well enough that you can speak without your notes. I have found it helpful to have a file of stories or illustrations that are easily remembered that I can share as a final word of comfort.[3]

Pall Bearers and Others

The funeral home staff will handle the pall bearers but you should make a point of thanking them for their service. You should also thank whoever participated in the service, as well as those who performed military honors.

After the Funeral

Do not just leave the family. You may or may not attend a dinner with the family following the funeral. Many churches still provide a luncheon. It is much appreciated by the family. If it is your church you should probably attend the dinner. If you do not know the family very well you could encourage them to share the time with their family and friends and not concern themselves with entertaining you, as you are an outsider to most of them. Over the years I have been using a specific follow–up plan, a series of booklets entitled

---

3 Appendix C has committal ideas that families have appreciated.

Journey Through Grief.[4] There are four booklets in the set sent at three weeks, three months, six months, and one year after the death. Each one includes a letter to accompany the booklet. I changed the letters to be personal from me. Families have consistently thanked me for them.

You need to understand one important thing. Funerals take a lot of time and you would like to be compensated for it. You have a right to be paid, but do not expect that you will be compensated every time. Usually the funeral director will take care of it for the family. You may wish to discuss your expectations with funeral directors. Sometimes they don't understand how much time you put into the whole funeral event. If you have a secretary you can ask her/him to inform families who contact you through her/him what you believe is fair. If the family asks you, answer them. Yes, you will feel like a mercenary but they ask because they want to treat you fairly and they do not know what is fair. They will not be upset when you tell them. If you do not get compensated, *do not* send a bill. Just accept it and move on. Do not hold a grudge. Maybe they thought the funeral service provider was taking care of you and the funeral director thought they were. Whatever the reason, it was not meant to insult you. It will balance out when a different family pays you very handsomely for a funeral you do for them.

One Last Thought

On March 30, 1981 I was gathered with friends to watch the championship game of the NCAA Men's Basketball Tournament. Most of the men I was with worked for our local newspaper, including the lead writers and managing editor. When news broke that President Ronald Reagan had been shot, I expected them to run to the office to prepare for the next day's paper. While they did get excited and discussed their plans, only one writer left the game.

---

4   Haugk, *Journey Through Grief.* These booklets can be found at Stephen Ministries, http://stephenministries.org/On_Line_Store

They already had prepared an obituary and other articles to run in the paper for just such happenings. Documents are prepared for just about every important person for whom they might need special newspaper editions. I learned the value of preparing ahead of time for people for whom I expect to lead a funeral. It seems a bit macabre but I keep a file for individuals with ideas, thoughts, anecdotes and remembrances. This way I am already partially prepared. Funerals seldom come at convenient times. If you are prepared the funeral will be less of a burden on you. If you follow these steps as you work through the process of each funeral you will bless families in grief.

Chapter Two
A Successful Wedding is in the Details

As pastors we have the privilege of officiating weddings. This is a great ministry opportunity and we should use it to good advantage. A well–done wedding will attract people to your church. In my church of around 110 families, about thirty were couples whose weddings I performed. With the privilege comes responsibility. Many people choose to be married by a pastor rather than a law clerk or Justice of the Peace so adjudge it a responsibility to perform weddings. With that you will need to consider some questions in your own mind.

- Will you serve couples not affiliated with your church?
- Does your denomination or congregation have restrictions on whom you can marry?
- Does your congregation have rules governing the use of the building?
- Will you officiate a wedding outside of the church building?
- Will you officiate weddings for non-Christian couples?

- Will you marry individuals who were previously divorced?

- And of course, will you perform a wedding for a same sex couple?

I have decided these issues in my mind and will leave it to you to decide for yourself. This book is not intended to establish theological positions. It is a "How To" guide. That said, I encourage you to think through these issues and establish your own protocols before you start doing weddings. You will get requests from all kinds of couples in all kinds of situations, so have your response prepared. Once you have constructed your guidelines put them on paper. This will enable you to give a ready answer to a request. If you have an administrative assistant who fields calls requesting your services you should communicate your principles to her/him.

People will often ask you what you charge, and you will feel usurious when you give a number, still you need to tell them what you expect. They want to pay you fairly but have no idea what fair is. Think about how much time you invest in a wedding. Let's say you do four or five sessions of counseling. How many hours of preparation and follow–up will you spend in addition to the counseling sessions themselves? How much time will you spend with the couple planning? How many hours will you spend preparing the wedding service, including your message? How many hours will the rehearsal take? How many hours will you spend preparing and cleaning up the chapel (unless you have staff or janitor who does it)? How many hours will you give to the wedding itself? I typically spent about 20 hours for a wedding not including counseling. How much are your twenty hours worth? How much is it worth for you to be away from your family for the rehearsal and the wedding, and possibly the reception? If you undervalue yourself people will seldom raise your price.

Now consider, how much will they pay a DJ for the reception? She/he will spend perhaps 6 hours total. Yes the equipment is expensive, but how much have you spent on books and education to get where you are?

When I retired in 2020 I was asking for $350 and felt I was being cheap. My executive assistant had a sheet with rules governing the use of the building, the charge for using the building (members of our church were not required to pay for using the building), and my fee. She would go over it with prospective couples and if they agreed and the church's and my calendars were clear, she would set it up.

Premarital Counseling

You will need to decide if you are going to require premarital counseling. Premarital counseling is extremely valuable but it is time consuming. If you are going to spend the time it should be worth every minute. I have found that some couples will agree to counseling only to get you to do their wedding, without putting real effort into it, not realizing the long term value. If a couple will not work with me, I may still do their wedding but it will be more like a law clerk or judge than a pastor. Either way I will make it personal and give them the best I can.

If you are going to do premarital counseling begin now to prepare what you will teach.[5] Do not be so rigid that you cannot adjust to fit the couple you are working with. Every couple is different and you will want to fashion your counseling to their relationship and needs. Most basic teaching about marriage will be valuable for every couple. Have some programs that you are comfortable working with, then create a plan for each couple you work with.

Planning the Wedding Ceremony

As you plan the wedding remember it is their wedding, not yours. Plan something that fits their goals and personalities. Most

---

5   Appendix D has ideas and teaching for premarital counseling.

states require only that the paperwork is signed by the couple and you, so you can be creative with the ceremony. Certainly there are traditions that may affect the wedding ceremony but they are probably not required. Encourage the couple to be mindful and respectful of their families while doing it their way.[6] The more simple the plan the less chance for noticeable mistakes in the wedding itself.

If you have not already determined what you are willing to do and what you are not willing to do in a wedding ceremony, do so before you meet with the couple. They do not want to hear you say no to their ideas unless you have a clear reason. Again, it is their wedding so help them do it their way.

Some people, especially brides, will already have an idea of what they want the wedding to look like. Your role is to help them make it work. It helps to have a basic outline of the elements of a wedding and how they follow from one to the next. As you introduce and discuss each element, guide them to organize the elements so that the ceremony flows seamlessly.

The basic elements of a typical wedding are: Processional(s); Invocation; Giving of the Bride; Music; Readings; Homily; Exchange of Vows; Exchange of Rings; Prayer for the Couple/Blessing; Official Pronouncement; Wedding Kiss; Introduction of Husband and Wife; Recessional; Receiving line. We will consider these elements individually.

Processional(s). Many weddings include three processionals. First is family, grandparents, siblings, mothers of the bride and parents of the groom. I tried to arrange the processionals always with the bride as the center of attention. The groom's family would enter before the bride's family for example: groom's grandparents; bride's grandparents; groom's siblings; bride's siblings; groom's parents; bride's mother. You may have to be creative when one or both of the

---

6   Appendix E is a sheet of basic information (with explanations) that I get from the couple early in the planning process.

couple come from divorce situations with stepmothers and stepfathers. Of course not all weddings include a family processional.

The second processional is the bride's maids and groom's men. Some couples want the men to enter separately from the women. The men proceed to the front of the venue and meet the women as they enter, then take the platform together. Some will want them entering as couples. Perhaps the men will meet the women at the aisle and escort the women to the front. There is no rule on this so let them do it their way.

The formation of the wedding party on the platform is entirely up to the couple and the venue. If men and women stand on opposite sides of the couple, symmetry makes for nice photos. If they stand as couples, seek balance if possible.

If someone asks where they should focus their attention, suggest that they watch whoever is acting, be it the next member of the wedding party or a musician. Other than that, ask them to focus on the bride.

The final processional is the entrance of the bride. This is when you encourage the guests to stand. The bride will usually be escorted by her father or someone else who is significant to her. If there is a flower girl or ring bearer or both, have them precede the bride down the aisle. The bride and her father stop at the front of the aisle and pause for you to welcome guests and offer a prayer. Then you ask, *"Who brings this woman to be married to this man?"* or whatever wording you and the couple choose. After that, the groom and bride follow you to the platform.

Sometimes at this point the couple will choose to honor their mothers in some way such as giving them each a rose or some other gift. It is a touching and emotional moment. If they choose to do so, guide them in how to go about it.

Invocation. Most couples, even if they are not Christians will appreciate a prayer as you begin the ceremony. You don't need to preach in this prayer. Simply pray for God's blessing on the couple.

Giving of the Bride. Most couples still ask for a giving of the bride. I usually asked, *"Who brings this woman..."* rather than *"Who gives this woman..."* After all it is not an arranged marriage. The couple chose each other. The bride's father may answer however he and the bride agree.

Music. Whether it be an organ, piano, guitar, string quartet, or recorded music, most weddings include some music. Usually there is music of some sort as prelude while guests gather and take seats. This is the couple's choice. I encourage them to select music that they like.

Many couples today do not have a friend or relative to play or sing live music and may request the church organist or pianist. If so you should help them arrange it and make sure she/he is remunerated. They may choose to use recorded music. If so help them choose songs that are appropriate for processional and recessional. I kept recorded music, including many traditional and commonly used wedding songs that the couple could choose from if they did not have something specific in mind.

They may wish to have a friend or relative sing a particular song in the ceremony. Live music adds beauty to the event. However I encouraged them to use people who can sing. Someone who is great at karaoke is not necessarily a good singer in a context away from a karaoke bar. A bad singer can distract from the beauty of the wedding. Be diplomatic but do your best to encourage that they find a gifted singer.

Readings. Many couples will ask to have a friend or relative share a reading of some sort such as a scripture or poem. Try to make sure the reading to be used is appropriate and encourage the reader to practice. He or she needs to be well prepared so that, when under the scrutiny of a microphone, she or he does not choke up. Encourage her/him to prepare the reading in printed form using large font because her/his eyes may be tear–filled from the emotion of the event.

Homily. Although a homily is not necessary for a wedding most couples are happy for you to speak to them for a few minutes. Keep it short. Nobody wants to stand for a lengthy sermon. Speak about marriage. It is not a gospel presentation. Understand that the couple will remember very little of what you say. On the other hand, the guests will be tuned in and will respond to you later if your message was meaningful. Be personal but not embarrassing. Humor is acceptable but use it carefully. It is not a roast. If the couple are Christians, offer a message from a Biblical perspective. Keep a collection of ideas.[7]

Exchange of Vows. Even vows are not required by law. From my perspective they are the most important part of the ceremony. I encouraged the couple to choose vows carefully, whether they write personal vows or use something traditional. This is the promise they bring to the marriage. Encourage them to choose vows that will be the promise they give to the other. I challenged them to regularly review their vows to measure themselves by their promise. I would go over the words of the vows with each of the couple before we get to the wedding. It helps them feel more comfortable about speaking them in front of the congregation.

In every wedding I performed the couple promised something like *"until death do us part"*. I talk with them about the permanence of that promise and how in their vows they promise that their love will continue even if their circumstances change. These heavy and

---

7   Appendix F has examples of homilies.

serious promise are often forgotten when life does not live up to an image they hold.[8]

While planning the wedding I gave the couple a copy of options for choosing vows and encourage them to study them carefully, choosing vows that say what they intend to promise. They can use something as written or mix and match, or even write something new from the ideas included. If they choose to write their own vows, remind them to put them in typed form with large font that is easily read with tears in their eyes. Also, remind them to practice reading their vows because sometimes they will write ideas that are difficult to actually speak.

Again, emphasize the importance of the vows they will promise in their wedding. After the wedding I give the couple a copy of the entire wedding, encouraging them to read their vows every year on their anniversary. I ask them to examine themselves to see if they are living up to what they promised. I point out that if they are, they are probably also enjoying a wonderful marriage.

Exchange of Rings. As with the vows, what is said during the ring exchange is very important. Give them options of what to say.[9]

Before the ceremony I would have both the bride and groom practice out loud what they will say during the ceremony. Make sure they are comfortable speaking the words. In the ceremony, if their vows are *"repeat after me"* I would break the vows into short phrases so that it is not necessary for them to memorize anything. They are often scared and ill–at–ease speaking before a crowd. Make it easy for them.

Discuss who will hold the rings before they are exchanged in the ceremony. I found that it works well to have the Best Man hold the rings. When I called for them I asked him to place them on my palm. I then would make a statement about the meaning of the rings. Next

---

8   Appendix G offers examples of vows I have used or gathered from weddings I have attended.

9   Appendix H includes examples.

I would ask the groom to go first in putting the ring on his bride's finger. He would take the ring from my palm. In this there was no finger to finger contact which lessened the risk of fumbling. This made it less likely that someone would drop a ring. If a ring was dropped I asked for the Best Man to retrieve it.

Prayer for the Couple/Blessing. You may choose to have a moment to offer your special blessing on the couple. As an agent of Christ, say something personal to the couple. If you pray, pray about the couple and nothing else.

Official Pronouncement. At this point the ceremony is nearly over. They have offered their promises (vows) and received them from each other, sealed with rings. They are essentially married. Everything that is marriage is now in place. The official pronouncement is merely you declaring what has just happened.

Couple's Communion. If the couple are Christians and, depending on the traditions of their church or denomination, this is a good time for them to declare that Jesus Christ will be the center of their marriage. I often would lead the couple in a private communion service. This makes their first act as a married couple an act of worship. After a short explanation I served the bread and wine to the groom and allowed him to serve his wife. This is a very effective illustration of what God desires of them.

Wedding Kiss. This is seldom the first time the couple will kiss so I usually said to the groom something like, *"Someone should kiss this bride."* I did once have a groom who had not yet kissed his bride before this moment so truly it fit to say, *"You may now kiss the bride!"*

Introduction of Husband and Wife. Now you enjoy the privilege of being the first person ever to introduce *"Mr. and Mrs. John and Jane Doe."*

Recessional. The bride and groom and wedding party now egress the platform. I have them do so in reverse order from the processional, including the parents and maybe the rest of their families.

Receiving Line. Some couples will want to receive their guests immediately following the ceremony, especially those guests who will not be attending the reception. I discourage from having the entire wedding party as part of this receiving line. Having them participate can make for a very long experience. I encourage the wedding party to relax, perhaps get a drink of water, and prepare for photos.

There are other elements that can be added to the ceremony depending on the couple's desire and historical traditions, e.g. Unity Candle; Mixing Sand; Jumping the Broom.[10]

Once the plan is completed I would send a typed copy of the service outline to them. They could review it and agree or not. They may also intend to create a printed program to give to guests so this would assist them.

The Rehearsal

You will do the family a great favor by leading a succinct and focused rehearsal. If possible take charge of the rehearsal immediately. Some churches use a staff member or wedding coordinator to lead rehearsals. I preferred to lead them myself. If the wedding venue is somewhere other than your church building you may be restricted by the rules of the host building. You are the one leading the wedding so make sure everyone knows what you and the couple have planned. There will be lots of suggestions from others of what should be done and how. I have a friend who does not allow mothers, especially of the bride, at the rehearsal. It is up to you to make sure the couple enjoys the wedding they planned.

---

10 Appendix I has examples of what to say for some common elements.

When setting the time for the rehearsal, point out that they should determine when their wedding party can be present. There is no sense in holding a practice without the participants. You want the father of the bride, any musicians, singers, readers, and anyone else who will be actively participating including a DJ to be present. On the night of rehearsal arrive early so that you can welcome everyone. If the location is somewhere you are not familiar with being early will allow you to become comfortable and anticipate any changes that might be necessary to make the plan work.

Rehearsal should not be a drawn out affair. Make it an enjoyable experience. I began with just the bride and groom. I talked through the wedding to be sure what we have on paper is what they want. There may be changes that they decided upon after the planning. That's OK. You can change anything right up until you begin the wedding itself. Talk about where the wedding party will stand. Notice if you will need voice or music amplification and if so where the equipment needed will be located.

When everyone has arrived, gather them all together and introduce yourself. Ask the bride and groom to introduce their family and friends present. I usually offered a short prayer asking God to help us focus and remember tomorrow what we have rehearsed tonight.

Now talk through the ceremony with everyone. Have the wedding party, singers, and musicians stand where they will be during the wedding. If possible, with small pieces of masking tape, mark the location of each one. Ask those present who are not part of the platform to comment on how the platform looks from the congregation's point of view. As incentive for young children to remember and follow the plan, I often would mark their spots with a dollar coin which I told them they can keep after the wedding.

Now walk through with music. This allows everyone to be comfortable with timing in accordance with the music chosen. Be aware, if processional music is provided by a string trio or quartet, they will usually play the whole song even if it is longer than necessary to get everyone into position. It is much easier for a pianist or single guitar player to cut a song short than it is for a trio or quartet. If they are using a DJ, ask her/him to fade the song out as opposed to just hitting the stop button. If the wedding venue includes a raised platform it is important that you talk about the potential of tripping while ascending stairs, especially if the women are wearing heels. I encouraged the men to offer an arm until the women are at the level they will hold during the ceremony.

The singers and readers do not have to practice their roles during rehearsal but practicing their movement is helpful. They may choose to practice once or twice in the setting.

You may need to try two or three times. You will learn that the more simple the wedding you have planned, the easier it is for everyone and requires no memorization. The wedding party need only know when to move, where to move to, where to stand, and when to move out. If they are going up and down stairs and the women will be wearing heels remind the men to offer an arm so that no one trips and you all end up on TV or internet videos.

There are certain other things to cover at rehearsal. Discuss with ushers what to do plus how and when. They may also be escorting family in the processional and recessional. If they are seating guests, remind them to keep things balanced. I once did a wedding in which the groom's family was new to town and had no guests. Everyone sat on the bride's side until it was full and only then did anyone sit on the groom's side but way in the back. Many couples today ask their guests to choose a seat not a side. Encourage the ushers to find a comfortable place to sit during the ceremony.

Talk about the receiving line. By now you and the couple have determined who will be standing in this line so you do not need everyone else in this discussion.

Make sure everyone knows, if there are children in the wedding (flower girl and/or ring bearer), they may not do what you planned.

Even if they practiced it perfectly, it may be different when there is a crowd watching them. They may become show–offs. Then again, they may just run to Mom or Grandma. Tell everyone not to make a fuss. Let kids be kids. The more everyone tries to get them to do something, the less likely they are to do it and that distracts from the wedding.

Talk to the best man about his responsibilities. Because the best man usually holds the rings before the exchange, ask him where they will be. Make sure they are easily retrievable. Talk to him about placing them in your palm. I also asked the best man to take charge if something goes wrong. If someone faints everyone knows that he will react. If a ring is dropped ask him to be the one to pick it up. Anyone else should only point out the location. The women do not need to be crouching down in heels and a dress and you do not want two people banging heads scrambling for the ring.

The last thing I did was remind everyone that only we know what is supposed to happen and when. Tell them if they make a mistake, act like they meant it and make a correction. No one else will know.

The Wedding Day

Arrive early. Make sure everything is ready. Read through your notes or manuscript for the ceremony, including your homily. Go over everything with the bride and groom. Many couples do not want the groom to see his bride in her wedding gown until she enters the sanctuary so you may have to do this separately. Pray with each of them if possible. Help them each practice their speaking parts.

Connect with the DJ or musicians, and a sound technician if they have one. Make sure everyone knows the plan. Check your microphone(s). Reread your notes. It is helpful to provide an outline of the ceremony for musicians, DJ, readers, etc. This will help them be ready when it is their time to act. It is also helpful to give a copy to the photographer and wedding coordinator if there is one. After the ceremony make a point of speaking with everyone who partici-pated in the ceremony, thanking them for their help.

Usually there will be posed photos taken after the guests have departed. You may wish to ask the photographer to take any that include you (e.g. with the bride and groom) quickly so you can take care of other things while they complete taking photos.

It is very important that you make sure the legal documents are signed. You are responsible for these. If they are missed or done incorrectly you will be responsible to correct them. I generally also took responsibility to send the legal papers to the Clerk of Courts myself. That way I did not have to worry about these documents getting lost in the gathering of belongings or forgotten from the reception and honeymoon. Make copies of them in case something does get lost. Make a few extra copies of the legal marriage doc-ument to give to the bride for use if she is changing her name on driver's license and Social Security registration. Some clerks will refuse copies and require an original that the couple must get from the Clerk of Courts.

Often when the couple applies for the marriage license they are given a Marriage Certificate that is not required but the couple may wish to have framed. Witnesses are not usually required to sign the legal documents however, it is nice if you have the Maid of Honor and Best Man sign the certificate as witnesses. If you are filling this out make sure your handwriting is clear and legible. I usually found someone with very nice penmanship to help me with this. Some couples will include signing their papers as part of the ceremony. If so, be prepared with a good pen.

If you are in charge of the building you will need to be around until photos are finished and everyone has left for the reception. Check to make sure, as much as possible, that they have taken all of their personal items such as clothes, hair and make–up supplies, as well as whatever might have to be returned to a rental agency.

Before they leave, give a copy of the ceremony to the couple. I usually gave the copy to the bride's mother (or another person that is dependable) and asked that she get it to the couple. I again encouraged them to keep it in a safe place and read their vows every year on their anniversary. Keep a copy for yourself. You might be surprised how often you want to look at what you did in previous weddings, especially if you are reusing certain ideas.

Photos

During planning I ask the couple what, if any, restrictions they want. Some do not want photos taken during the ceremony. Everything can be recreated later. You may have personal restrictions. It is important that the photographer not distract from the ceremony. Professional photographers usually know how to seem invisible. Amateurs usually do not.

Professionals know what pictures to take and have probably already worked it out with the couple. Amateurs seldom do. I have found it helpful to provide a list of potential photos I picked up from a professional many years ago. I made a point of giving a copy to the couple during our planning sessions. Even if they have a professional, they may find something in that list that they want that is not on the professional's list.[11] One photo that often gets missed until I call attention to it is when the couple sign their papers.

Fee

Sometimes you will not get paid your fee. You are not doing this to get rich but it is nice to be compensated for your time and effort. If no one pays you, do not send a bill. Do remember that you are responsible to be sure the church is paid for use of the building including janitor costs, and that musicians and singers get paid. Unless you provided a DJ, paying the DJ is the family's responsibility.

---

11   Appendix J is the list of photo ideas I gave the couple.

The Reception

For several years I was averaging ten weddings each year. I already gave the couple my time counseling and planning. I gave them the night before the wedding for rehearsal. If I attended every rehearsal dinner and reception, that equals twenty evenings in a year away from my wife and kids. The family will invite you to rehearsal dinner and reception. It is the polite thing to do. Unless they are friends whose wedding I would have attended even if I were not the officiant, I politely declined. Instead I encouraged them to enjoy celebrating with their family and friends.

If you are attending the reception ask someone to save a seat for you and your wife if she is also going because you will probably be one of the last to arrive at the reception hall since you remained to close up the church building. You may find yourself sitting alone or at a table with no one you know.

It is good to own an in–style, well–fitting suit for weddings. The men in the wedding party will most likely be wearing suits or tuxedos and the women will be in their finest. You don't want to look like a rag–a–muffin. You may want to learn the colors the bride has chosen so that you can wear a tie that coordinates with her choice. Photos of the pastor in a fire engine red tie are conspicuously distasteful.

At the reception be conscious of your behavior. More than once I heard people talk about the foolish behavior of the pastor at the reception, or worse how drunk he got. Remember, you are always being watched. You represent Christ and there are many who look to you for how to live as a Christian in special situations.

Chapter Three
A Sermon Is More Than Words on a Page

Preaching is a calling and a ministry. It is also a job. In this chapter I will share thoughts about the job of preaching, that is, the work that you put into preaching. Work hard at this while remembering your focus. If in your sermon writing you seek to impress your listeners with you as a preacher, they will not be impressed with the Jesus you preach.

If you attended a Bible College or seminary you probably experienced at least one class in homiletics. You should be prepared to write and deliver good sermons. That is the art of preaching. This includes your own study habits, style, and presentation comfort. It is part of your calling. You will have perhaps a half hour each week to reach your largest audience with the message of the Word of God. Be the best preacher you can be. Do not stop learning and improving. Study the art of preaching. Listen to other preachers. Read the work of other preachers. Attend preaching seminars. Take classes at a local seminary. Improve. Improve. Improve. That is the job of preaching. So let us now consider certain issues of this job.

Establish your purpose

Each sermon you write has a purpose. Is it to teach, to challenge, to encourage, to convict, or maybe to entertain? Decide what your intent is for each sermon. That needs to be clear in your mind. It will affect how you develop your message, the outline and the kinds of illustrations you use. Every sermon is not for everyone. The truth is always true, but sometimes you write sermons for certain people or groups or about specific issues. Are you preaching to seekers, to new believers, or to long–time church members? Most of the time you will be speaking to all three. From time to time there will even be skeptics. Seeker oriented sermons will not challenging long–time Christians. On the other hand, deep theological Bible studies will be difficult for new believers who lack background. Determine who a sermon is primarily intended for and adjust parts of it to serve the others as well.

Special occasions call for special sermons. Major historical events (September 11, 2001, the assassination of a major political figure, a momentous natural disaster), changes in church direction, special campaigns (building program), transition of leadership or setting aside new leaders and ordaining new ministers all call for special words from you. When a church loses an important and influential member a special sermon should be considered. Certainly holidays call for sermons to be reflective (Christmas, Resurrection Sunday, Mother's Day). You will have to consider all of this carefully. It may affect how you plan your preaching calendar.

Involve your church leaders or staff into this planning. Usually they will agree with your plans but it is good to hear their input and they will appreciate being heard. What and how you preach will have a huge impact on your church's membership and growth.

Length of Sermons

Some preachers who are naturally entertaining can get away with long sermons. People like to be entertained but let us never forget, we are presenting the Word of Almighty God. Go into show business if you want to entertain

Most of us should be conscious of the length of our sermons. This is congregation dependent and there is no perfect length. Even while some of your audience have long attention spans, others do not. However long you choose to preach, make it worth the time of your listeners. No one wants to feel like they have wasted a half hour listening to drivel. As I wrote in chapter one, *"It is a sin to be boring in preaching."*

You will find it much more difficult to write short sermons that honestly cover the issue than long sermons filled with palaver. Publishers like lots of words in a book. Congregations do not. Avoid using a lot of unnecessary words in a sermon. Make every word meaningful. Invest the time to write sermons that are filled with solid Biblical teaching but not with unnecessary verbiage.

Style

There is no right style for preaching. Great preachers in history and in contemporary Christianity use all kinds of styles: conversational; lecture; loud; soft; story–telling; arguing from Scripture. Some are very formal, some are homey and casual. You will establish your own style. It is acceptable, even recommended, that you vary your style occasionally. None–the–less you will have your own style. Work with it. Be creative.

Content

This is very important. Your sermon could be nothing more than a service league presentation if it lacks good Biblical content. It may be true and may be helpful, but if it is not the Word of God, it is just you spouting your ideas. If you choose to teach something you believe to be right and good that is not necessarily taught in scripture, make it clear that this is your thinking, not the Word of God.

Do the work of studying every text so that you know the material before using it.[12] Make sure every text says what you are using it for. Do not try to make the text say what you want it to say. For example, how many times have you heard someone use *"Where there is no vision the people perish,"*[13] to promote a church's vision statement? Vision statements are great but that text is about having a Word from God. Where there is no Word from God people perish. Another often misused example is, *"Train up a child in the way he should go and when he is old he will not depart from it."*[14] That text actually says, *"Train up a child in his way . . ."* Do you see how that changes the purpose of the text? Do not proof text. Do the work to know what each Bible reference you use means.

Let the text drive your sermons. Again, this is not a speech for Kiwanis. You are speaking on behalf of God Himself. Study the text and use it to determine the point of your sermon. This is the difference between preaching yourself, what you think, and what God has said. Your preaching then is *"the wisdom that comes from heaven"* of which James wrote.[15]

Verify the accuracy of the illustrations you use. You will know people are listening when you share an illustration but it is wrong. Someone will talk to you about it afterward. Get numbers and dates correct. Someone will know the right date or number and will correct you. Often she/he will focus on that mistake for the rest of your talk thus missing the point of the illustration or even the entire sermon. You will know because you will be immediately approached and corrected after the service. That is just the way people are. Get it right. If you are using a story do your best to be certain it is true. If you are not sure, let it be known. Remember Jesus told stories

---

12 Gregory, *Seven Laws of Teaching*. Originally published in 1886 it is still in print and can be downloaded. Read it often. Law One begins, "The teacher has got to know the material."

13 Proverbs 29:18

14 Proverbs 22:6

15 James 3:17

that were not true, parables, that none–the–less helped His listeners understand God's Word.

Learn how to pronounce names. Practice if necessary. Some Biblical names can be difficult. Take the time to say them correctly. Do not excuse the laziness of not learning how to pronounce names and words. A good Bible dictionary will help you learn proper pronunciation.

Be contemporary with illustrations. Certain "old" illustrations have been used ad nauseam, for example the Blondin tight roping across Niagara Falls story. How many times must we hear about the guy on his roof during a flood refusing rescue by boats and helicopter? If you are not good at creating interesting and effective illustrations (most of us are not) find good sources. You may have to check the veracity of some of what you find. Do it. Give credit to your source and when you use the illustration, use it like it was your own.

Finding ideas for sermons and sermon series

Of course you have in your hands the greatest source of ideas, your Bible. You cannot go wrong allowing God's Word to lead your sermons. That being said, most of us like to use, and people like to hear, creative ways of teaching the Bible. You do not have to reinvent the wheel. *"There is nothing new under the sun,"*[16] not even in preaching. There is no shame in getting ideas from other preachers. Sermoncentral.com is an excellent resource but be careful that you do not simply use another's work without giving credit.

Read. Read. Read. Read books of sermons by some of the greats. The writings of A.W. Tozer will spark ideas in your mind and inspire ideas for sermons. So also Jonathan Edwards, Billy Graham, Charles H. Spurgeon, Harry Emerson Fosdick, John Stott, Martin Lloyd Jones. There are many contemporary preachers that will inspire ideas for you. Many great sermon series have been built

---

16 Ecclesiastes 1:9

on a book written by a trusted author. If you use an author's book as a starting point, especially if you use the outline of a book, give the author credit. Do not simply copy another's work. If you are going to copy what someone else has written you would do just as well to read the book to your congregation. After acknowledging your source, make it yours.

Devotionals, journals, and podcasts are also great sources of inspiration. Listen and take notes. If you find a particular preacher that you connect with, such as Chuck Swindoll, James Kennedy, or David Jeremiah, learn from him or her. When using ideas be sure that you are preaching the Bible and not that preacher.

Create a filing system for good ideas. In *Ordering Your Private World*[17], Gordon MacDonald offers ideas about keeping and sorting good ideas.

Many preachers plan their sermons well in advance, some for as much as a year at a time. There is no right way to plan. Find what works for you and use it.

Know what you are saying

One of the fundamental laws of teaching is that you as the teacher must know what you are teaching. Too many preachers write sermons filled with good material, but with no focus. You have to have a clear picture of the point of your sermon. On the first day of my first doctoral seminar the professor asked each of us in the class to tell him in one sentence what we preached the day before. Because I have always made this part of my sermon writing, I was able to respond satisfactorily.

After you have studied the text, not before, determine what you plan to teach from it. Write in one sentence what the point of your sermon is. Do not start with your idea and search for a text to support it. Let the text drive the sermon. Write it out and keep it handy

---

17   MacDonald, *Ordering Your Private World.*

as you compose the sermon. I call this sentence my "Big Idea Statement."[18] Not original but useful. It will usually go through several iterations before you have finished the sermon.

Writing a Big Idea Statement is hard work but well worth the effort. This single sentence Big Idea Statement offers several benefits. It will help you craft your outline. Because you know what you plan to say, this sentence will help you organize how you will say it. It determines your sub-points, each of which needs to support this purpose sentence. You will never go blank in the pulpit if you have prepared well.

Your Big Idea Statement will help as you seek ways to illustrate your point. You will know what thought the illustration must support. Throughout your sermon every part should flow from and/or support your Big Idea Statement.

Your Big Idea Statement will also help when you are using ideas that you gained from a book or another preacher. Sometimes that great idea you found in a book does not really fit what you are saying. The idea may need to be tweaked some in order to support your Big Idea. You can only do that if you know your Big Idea.

Sermon Series

Writing sermons in series can be quite helpful. It helps advance preparation because as you study for one sermon you are also studying for subsequent messages. Also, as you work on each sermon, ideas come that may not fit this particular message but can be used later. Before you start the series determine the Big Idea of the series then be sure each sermon supports the main idea of the series.

There is no "right" length for a series, however I encourage you to regularly take the pulse of your congregation to see that they are still interested. It is possible for you to wear out the idea before you

---

18   Professor John Webb taught this in homiletics class at Minnesota Bible College.

have finished your plan. Whatever your plan, be sure to allow room for interruptions. You just don't know when some major event (a natural disaster or a particularly egregious crime in your community) will come along that you should address. Do not ignore such an event because you already planned something else.

In the pulpit

Let's discuss a little bit about the presentation of your well–written sermons. Practice out loud. Make sure you are comfortable with every word you plan to speak. It is easy to write something that your tongue cannot say without getting tied in a knot. You want your message to flow from your mouth easily. Learn to pronounce the words you will speak. If you are not sure look them up before you go to the pulpit. Enunciate. *"dis"* and *"dat"*, *"woulda"* and *"coulda"*, and the like make you sound uneducated. Avoid seeking feedback by saying *"You know"*. That tends to be an irritant to many people. You want your congregation to trust your ability as a student.

Try not to use slang. You do not have to speak like an English gentleman, however you should realize that slang (short–language) does not always mean the same thing to others as it does to you.

Be careful about using generalities and superlatives. *"We all wish we had more money."* Not necessarily. *"Americans no longer believe in God."* Probably not true. Probably most of the people in your congregation do believe in God. *"The most commonly quoted verse in the Bible."* How do you know that? *"The greatest, biggest, longest . . ."* Maybe. Maybe not. Do not say it unless you know for sure.

I highly recommend writing a manuscript so that you have carefully thought through your transitions and main statements. You do not have to read the manuscript, but it will help keep you on target without wandering. It will also serve to bring you back if you do get off on a tangent. A manuscript will help prevent stammering and stumbling for words because you have already thought through what you want to say. A manuscript eliminates unnecessary pauses while you try to think of what comes next. A manuscript is also beneficial when someone asks for a copy of the sermon. Rough notes will not serve them well. They want everything you said, not just the ideas you spoke from. When you have a manuscript you will be able to offer a copy. A final thought about using a manuscript, you can be free to engage your congregation members before the worship service begins because you have your message completely prepared.

Most of us use some form of word processor for preparation. Use font large enough for you to read without bending your face down to the page. You are trying to make good eye contact with your listeners. You cannot do that while your face is buried in your notes. If you believe what you are teaching is important, as you should, you want to connect with your listeners in a way that they too know that you believe it is important. Good eye contact is extremely important.

I encourage using a type–written format on a printed page. Electronic technology is probably easier but it is risky. Electronics have a way of failing at the wrong time.

When reading from your Bible learn to pronounce every word and name. Do not get sloppy. Do not assume you will get it right as you preach unless you have practiced. Use a comfortable translation and be consistent. Do not choose a version because you like it. Too often preachers read a different translation than they usually use saying, *"I like the way this says it."* After you have studied the text thoroughly enough to be sure it communicates what the author wrote, be certain that you are confident in the version you choose. I often used my own translation except for lengthy passages. Before you get to the pulpit mark pages in your Bible. Do not fumble through your Bible looking for your text.

Turning the pages of your manuscript can be distracting so learn how to move from page to page effortlessly. Also number your pages in case you drop your notes or a sudden wind blows them off your pulpit.

Your church may record your preaching for broadcast or a You Tube type sharing platform. If not, periodically video record yourself preaching. Then watch it. You will learn a lot about your presentation. You will see your distractive habits and idiosyncrasies. You can often be your best critic.

How you dress for preaching depends on your congregation. Know your audience. You represent God in a very significant way. Respect the calling. How you dress should honor Him. Casual is not wrong but trying to be *"acceptable to non–believers"* is no reason to dress down. Consider what our society considers acceptable for leaders. When was the last time you saw a TV interview with a company CEO or government spokesman dressed in blue jeans with holes in the knees? Especially for women, be sure the way you dress does not create distraction. Modesty is key. Male listeners especially are distracted by a woman dressed in a sexy manner.

Dealing with critics

You will have critics. You cannot stop it. Even Jesus and Peter and Paul had critics. Be polite and listen to their concerns. Learn something if you can but trust your work and knowledge. How you respond to a critic can win him over to your faithfulness to God's Word. If you are easily offended or defensive you will probably cause him to turn from your preaching. *"A gentle answer turns away wrath."*[19] We probably all get frustrated with too much criticism so find a friend with whom you can vent without taking it out on the critic.

Using humor

Humor can be very effective in getting a message across but it can be easily misused merely for entertainment. All humor should support your Big Idea and should be tasteful. Do not tell jokes for

---

19   Proverbs 15:1

the joke's sake. Many preachers are naturally funny and their humor assists the delivery of the message. If you are not good at humor learn to be or do not use it.[20]

Index Your Sermons

It is wise to index your sermons so that you can retrieve a specific sermon in the future. It will serve you when you are asked to preach on a specific topic. Your sermon can also be used in teaching situations with only minor changes. Good teaching is good teaching. Make the most of what you have prepared.

The preacher's authority

When you preach, preach with authority. When Jesus taught, his listeners were impressed because, *"he taught as one who had authority and not as their teachers of the law"*.[21] No you are not Jesus and you do not have his authority but keep in mind that you are presenting the Word of God. You have worked hard to know the text. When you preach the Bible you are preaching with the calling and authority of God. Be bold.

Finally, understand, a great preacher is not one who writes great sermons. A great preacher is one who loves his congregation greatly.

---

20   John Branyon, an excellent Christian comedian, offers a short course in using humor in preaching. John@johnbranyan.com or http://johnbranyan.com/comedy-consultant/
21   Matthew 7:29

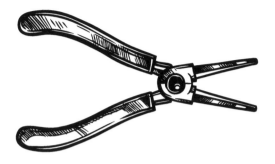

Chapter Four
Helping Church Members When They Are Hurting

This chapter is about practical considerations for your pastoral counseling. If you attended a Bible college or Christian seminary you probably experienced at least one class on counseling. If you did not, you should. Find a college or seminary that will allow you to attend a class because you will be called on to counsel church members. Assuming that you have done some study in counseling, here are some thoughts.

Where

You will need a place to meet with folks who are struggling and request your help. It may be your office or even in your home. Be sure your location is private but also not so isolated that you can be accused of something inappropriate. If you are counseling the opposite sex be sure you are not alone in the building and never close your door unless you have someone stationed right outside who can testify that you did nothing wrong. An accusation, even if false, can ruin your ministry. You might consider a door with a window. I would often ask our executive assistant to be present in the building when I was meeting with a woman.

Show utmost discretion when counseling someone of the opposite sex. Do not meet at a coffee shop or the like. Yes it is comfortable and is public but you risk someone misunderstanding why you are with him/her. It may look like a date. Also, the coffee shop lends itself to developing intimacy you do not intend. Many pastors have created trouble for themselves in such a way.

When

Counseling should not be allowed to take you away from your family too often. You have office hours. No they are not always convenient for others but your family must come first. Set a limit how often you will counsel outside of office hours. If you do not you can quickly become distant from your family, especially if you add in premarital and wedding preparation counseling. You must keep control of your calendar.

How long

There is no right length for a counseling session or number of sessions. You will have to determine length with each case but be careful not to go too long. After a while in a session you will usually begin to simply repeat the same things you talked about an hour ago. That is when it is time to end this session and schedule another.

Too many sessions can become a problem as well. The counselee may become dependent on you, unable to move forward on his/her own. Unless you are a certified counselor, anyone who needs long term counseling should see a professional. Have a list of professionals you can recommend. When you refer a church member, make it clear that you are not "dumping" her/him. You are doing your best by referring to someone who can provide better help. You will get criticized but better that than leading her/him on without real improvement. Before referring, know to whom you are referring. Research who you are recommending. Not every licensed counselor is going to be helpful.

Who

Determine who you are willing to counsel, whether church members or community members. Remember who is paying you. You will have friends or acquaintances who request your help. It can be a wonderful time to influence someone for Christ, but it does come with risk. Think this through before the request ever comes. Also be prepared for handling sensitive cases. You may be uncomfortable working with certain individuals. You will have to be careful when declining. It would be best to have a prepared statement of limits you hold to. I would also encourage you to establish your policy with the leaders of your church. What you do as the pastor of their church can affect them and their families. Individual Elders of a church have been caught up in law suits after the failure or even just a mistake by their pastor.

If you find yourself faced with someone who is struggling with gender dysphoria be very careful what you counsel. In some places in the world it is against the law to counsel such a one against "gender change."

Confidence

You must be able to maintain absolute confidence. There are few quicker ways to make people lose faith in you than to spread information you learned in counseling. Also remember that you are under laws governing the "confessional."

There is some doubt about which is weightier, counselor–client confidentiality or the obligation to report dangerous or illegal information to legal authorities. I recommend that you develop friendship with an attorney who can guide you through such cases, because at some time someone will confide in you that he has been abusive with his wife or child. You may establish at the beginning of a counseling relationship that you will keep confidence but in the case of some harmful or illegal confession confidentiality is suspended. Unless the counselee agrees to that, you may wish to refer.

It is a good idea to take and keep notes from counseling sessions. However, you must have a way to secure your notes. If someone were to break into your office, finding sensitive counseling notes could result in real hurt for your counselee.

As a pastor you will give a lot of teaching and advice in counseling. Give Biblical teaching and good advice, but realize that you can be taken to court if your advice does not prevent some negative action by a counselee. For example, you or your church can be sued for failing to prevent a suicide even if you offered the best advice. You have little protection in such a situation unless you are a certified professional. Refer this person to a professional if you are at all uncertain. Again, you will be criticized for it, still it is best for all involved and it is because you love her/him.

If you offer your opinion or advice about anything, always clarify that you are not a professional that specializes in the topic, unless you in fact are. For example, if you give an obese client advice about the benefits of diet and exercise, urge her/him to see a primary care provider before acting on your advice, and emphasize, *"I am not a physician or nutritionist. This is just an opinion based on my life experiences."*

Finally be sure you or your church carry insurance protection. Check with your agent. Usually a rider on your overall policy will be enough. I do not intend here to sound paranoid or extreme, however there are many examples of pastoral counselors who have had to fight charges of malpractice when a counselee experienced greater problems even after meeting with a pastor. You and your church can be dragged through court for years if you are not careful.

Chapter Five
I'm Not Musical. Can I Lead Meaningful Worship?

Who is responsible for the worship of the church? Whether your church has multiple staff including a worship minister or you are the sole hired staff using volunteer worship leaders, you are ultimately responsible. If you doubt this, pay attention the next time something major goes wrong in service or when someone changes *"the way we do things"*. Who do people complain to or about?

Realize that we live in a spectator society. People, even church people, want to watch a good show. They unconsciously compare your church to professionally–produced television, and your preaching to professional actors. I am not saying that worship is a show. I am saying that excellence in worship leadership has a positive effect on your congregation.

We have been given a lot of freedom of expression in worship and as the primary leader of the church you are responsible for the content and spirituality of worship. It is up to you to guide your church as a whole and as individuals to experience genuine personal worship.

At our church when leading worship we emphasized that we were on a platform. We discouraged the use of the word "stage". A stage is for performing, a platform is for leading. Our philosophy for leading was that our worship team and I worship and invite the congregation to worship with us. I routinely encouraged our people to raise their hands if they desired, or to stand or sit or kneel. We wanted each worship service to be a personal experience.

You may be the Lead Pastor of a large church that employs a professional worship leader who is responsible for song selection, musicians and singers, the use of arts, etc. You will still be expected to maintain meaning and dignity in worship. That is part of your leadership.

If you serve a small church you may well be the worship leader. You may feel uncomfortable singing in front of the group, especially if you are not confident in your singing ability. (More on this at the end of the chapter.) Remember, you are not singing to the congregation. You are singing to the God you worship. He is the only audience that matters. More than that, there are others in your congregation who are not good singers who will be emboldened that if you can do it so can they. You may actually assist non–singers to enjoy praising with songs, hymns, and spiritual songs.

Smaller churches who cannot employ someone for the role of worship leader often use volunteers who may or may not have specific theological training. You need to know what you believe is proper worship for your context. I am not suggesting that there is one specific style or method of worship that is right and others are wrong. You need to understand your church and lead in a style that fits the church membership. This will require you to determine the purpose of worship and what will fulfill that purpose.

Whether you choose a style that is traditional or contemporary, seeker sensitive or something designed for established Christians, "high" or "low" church, be sure your church accepts the style. I do not know who coined the phrase "worship wars" but as sad as it is, it is very descriptive of what happens when a pastor decides to change the style of worship without the membership's buy in. You may have been caught in just such a conflict. Worship wars are ugly, they hurt everyone, and put blemishes on Christ's bride. The best way to avoid them is to know what you believe is proper worship and lead your church accordingly.

It is not advisable to try to mix all kinds of styles in order to please everyone. That is very tricky and seldom successful. While you can get away with introducing elements from differing styles of worship, your church will probably not accept a different style each week. It is similar to radio stations. There are rock–n–roll, country, rap, classical, talk, etc. radio stations. Periodically a station may mix in something from a different style. If, for example, a rock station adds a song or two of classical genre, their listeners will usually forgive them. But a steady diet of a different style will send listeners to a different station. So it is with churches. Learn the style that works for your church and work with it. The key here is that you know what you believe the purpose of worship to be, then guide your church in it.

Modern technology provides many creative ways to express worship and it will continue to grow. If you are going to use technology, be sure to have a back–up plan for when the technology fails. How many times have you seen someone get up to speak trusting a computer or cell phone but it failed? The speaker says, *"I knew this would happen,"* and you are thinking, *"Then why did you use it?"* It is not unusual for a microphone or amplifier to fail, or for the mixing board to experience a glitch. Be prepared.

Consider the elements of worship your church uses. What is the purpose of each and how do they affect the overall purpose of worship. We took our lead from the New Testament starting with,

"They devoted themselves to the apostles' teaching and to the fellowship, to the breaking of bread and to prayer."[22]

I preached a sermon as part of each weekly worship experience because I believe that worship should help Christians grow in their knowledge and understanding of God (Apostles' teaching). I did not allow myself to think of the sermon as something I had to do each week, nor was it a time for me to pontificate. It was an opportunity for me to speak the heart and Word of God to our congregation and, as His spokesman, I did the work necessary to do my absolute best with each sermon. Yes, I offered some real bombs, but overall our congregation appreciated that I helped them know God's Word.

We emphasized relationships among our church members (fellowship) and encouraged taking time to share before and after worship services. Sometimes we included a time within the service for that specific purpose.

We also chose to celebrate The Lord's Supper (the breaking of bread) each worship service. We reminded our congregation that we were recognizing, honoring, and proclaiming the sacrifice Jesus made for our sins. We used a variety of individuals to offer meditation as part of the communion celebration. We found the freshness of the various approaches provided by the different speakers enhanced the experience for all of us. As always, I was responsible for what each speaker offered, thus I chose them carefully and provided guidance.

I believe one of the primary purposes of worship is to praise and honor Christ. To that end we chose to, *"speak to each other with psalms, hymns, and spiritual songs,"* and to *"make music in our hearts to the Lord"*.[23] Some songs specifically offered praise, some confession, some challenge or celebration. Each song was chosen to lift up Jesus Christ as Lord, Savior, and King. We regularly talked about the content of our songs and why we were singing them. We did not sing for the sake of singing even though our church loved to sing.

---

22   Acts 2:42
23   Ephesians 5:19

We pointed to our offerings as an element of worship as well, as through it we supported the work God called our church to. We did not make a big deal of "needing money." However, we regularly taught what the Bible says about tithing. Our members knew that our ministry was totally dependent on what we willingly gave to God.

Of course we included lots of prayer. We were careful to not let our prayers get too long. As one friend said to me, *"A long prayer is just a sermon with our eyes closed."* I consciously tried to avoid repeating the same things over and over in a given prayer. Jesus criticized pagans who, *"keep on babbling . . . for they think they will be heard because of their many words."*[24]

I encouraged our church to bring creative expressions of worship. We had a young woman who located herself in the back of the sanctuary and danced through the songs. She was careful not to distract others, but her love for Jesus flowed. Some people created banners and posters for us. Many worship leaders create specific "sets" on the platform to enhance a message or series. We did not. but only because we did not have the budget nor the volunteers it would require. Also, our platform barely had room for our worship band.

How long should a worship service be? There is no right answer to that question. However, I encourage you to take the pulse of your congregation. Pay attention to the responses of your congregation. If they are tuning out you are going too long. On the other hand, a too short service will have people asking why they bothered to come to church that day. Ask various people for their thoughts. Ask someone who you think might disagree with your leading. Most people will respect your leading if they know that you have heard concerns.

If you are thinking of making a major change in how your church does worship services, spend a lot of time talking to people

---

24   Matthew 6:7

about it. In order to avoid a "war" you will need to get buy–in from your church members. Back in the 1980s we took about a decade to transition from traditional (piano and organ leading older hymns) to contemporary worship with a guitar band. Only one family left our church as a result of the change. In fact we had more trouble getting the volume balanced than with the change of song style.

I caution you, although many if not most churches in America have gone to using contemporary hymns instead of the older hymns, do not say or even think, *"This isn't your Grandma's church anymore"*. It may not be, but Grandma still attends your church and that statement hurts her, making her feel unimportant and disrespected.

Finally, if you are uncomfortable leading the worship services of your church, and you do not employ a professional worship leader or have a willing servant whom you can teach the theology behind worship, it is up to you to lead. Please allow me to be transparent. I have always struggled with shyness. I get very nervous when that particular spotlight is on me, especially singing. For many years I was too self–conscious to be the lead voice in singing. Two things helped me overcome my weakness. First was when I studied the account of David bringing the Ark of the Covenant back to Jerusalem found in First Chronicles 13–15. In a much shorter account of this event we read that, *"David, wearing linen ephod, danced before the Lord with all his might while he and the entire house of Israel brought up the Ark of the Lord with shouts and sound of trumpets"*[25] He was criticized by his wife and others for his "lack of dignity", *"How the King of Israel has distinguished himself today, disrobing in the sight of the slave girls of his servants as any vulgar fellow would!"*[26]

David's response challenged me to rethink my fear of what people might think of me as I worshiped, *"It was before the Lord . . . when He appointed me ruler over the Lord's people Israel. I will celebrate before the Lord. I will become even more undignified than this, and*

25 Second Samuel 6:14–15

26 Second Samuel 6:20

I will be humiliated in my own eyes"[27] I came to realize what it means to worship before an audience of one. The congregation was not an audience, they were fellow sinners honoring our Savior. At this point I still could not say, *"I can dance in my underwear"* but I was moving in that direction.

The second thing that moved me the rest of the way to being a real worship leader happened in 1996 at a Promise Keepers Pastors Conference in Atlanta, GA. Jack Hayford was speaking of a humbling experience from several years before. He said he was in an airport and saw some children *"running in place and laughing."* Hayford said when parents told them to quit running they said that they weren't running, they were dancing, and he laughed at how silly they looked. He looked a bit silly himself demonstrating the "dance" for us. Sometime later he was in his private study worshiping God when he felt God calling him to dance. He resisted the feeling and thought, *"I don't know any dances to dance."* That is when God reminded him, *"Yes you do!"* With tears running down his cheeks, right there in his study, he began to run in place with his arms raised in praise to God. He then began running in place on that platform before a rapt audience. Seeing Jack Hayford running in place on the platform before thousands of dignified pastors, many of whom were also raising hands and running in place, I realized that in genuine worship one is not afraid even to look silly in someone else's eyes. Genuine, heart–felt worship is between the worshipper and God.

If you do not lead your congregation in personal worship, who will?

---

27   Second Samuel 6:21–22

Chapter Six
There Is a Ceremony for That

There will be times when you are called upon to lead special ceremonies. Some denominations have specific instructions for things like baptisms and ordinations. If your denomination does not or if you are from a non–denominational tradition you may have to develop your own format and style. Ideas can be gleaned from the Bible of what you might say in certain ceremonies, but mostly it will be up to you to create a format and text. In this chapter I will share some ideas and examples.

Baby Baptism/Dedication

I am part of a fellowship that does not do infant baptism, however we often do baby dedications. If your background uses infant baptism you can get help from a more experienced minister in how it is done. You can always call upon someone from another church for direction. Most denominations that do infant baptisms have a very specific formula for baptizing a baby.

Baby dedications are useful in churches that do not use infant baptism. They help new parents experience the emotions and pride of committing their child to Jesus. This can be done at regular intervals or when a number of new babies are born to your congregation. A baby dedication is in reality a dedication of and by the parents to raise their child in a Godly way with the help of the church. Parents are making a public statement of their personal commitment to lead their child to know Christ and one day accept him as personal Savior and Lord.

Meet with the parents prior to dedication to discuss the nature of the commitment they will be making in this ceremony. Go over the implication of the promise they will make before the church and before God. Go through the ceremony so that on dedication day they know what to expect. Point out that you will be asking the congregation to affirm their commitment to assist parents who dedicate their children by teaching them about Jesus.[28]

Create a printout of the ceremony including what each participant will say. Provide a copy for all who participate. Make this a nice document that the parents may cherish, for many will. Be sure to get baby names spelled correctly and during the ceremony pronounce their names correctly.

Baptism

For congregations that do not do infant baptism, there will be many opportunities for you to baptize adults, young adults, and children. It is up to you and your church to determine at what age you will baptize. The Bible does not talk of an age for baptism. Specific examples of baptisms in the New Testament describe people who have chosen to be baptized. For that reason I do baptisms for people who are of age to understand that they are making a decision for themselves. I allow the parents to determine if they are comfortable with their child making this choice. Then I meet with the

---

28 Appendix K offers a sample baby dedication.

child (with a parent or parents present) so that I am comfortable that he or she understands as much as possible what it means. I realize that many younger children are not capable of making a true "life" decision, but I never want to turn away a child who has made this decision. It then becomes the church's and my role to help that child continue that decision through the changes of growing up.

Some churches choose to have elaborate ceremonies for baptisms. One church regularly borrowed our facilities for an afternoon of baptisms, including singing and teaching as well as testimonies by these being baptized. Our church made baptism simple. As when the man from Ethiopia asked Phillip, *"Look, here is water. Why shouldn't I be baptized?"*[29] We do baptisms whenever someone chooses to be baptized. Our church had a heated baptismal. Wintertime baptisms can be mighty cold in northern Indiana so we usually scheduled baptisms for when we could first heat the water (it usually takes about a day and a half). However, if someone desired immediate baptism, we did it immediately.

As the New Testament does not require an age for baptism so it does not require a certain formula. We simply use the words from Peter's confession to Jesus at the "Transfiguration". We ask the person to declare that he or she believes that Jesus is the Christ the Son of the Living God.[30] If the person is comfortable enough to speak in front of people, especially when the baptism is part of a worship service, I asked him or her to repeat the following statement after me, broken into short phrases, *"I believe, that Jesus is the Christ, the Son of the Living God, and I accept Him, as my personal Savior and Lord"*. For the shy I put it in the form of a question and ask for an affirmative reply. Some churches welcome a testimony if the candidate desires to share. Video and audio enhancement to the congregation offers the one being baptized an opportunity to share her/his personal testimony. That may be the only time she/he every does so before

---

29   Acts 8:37
30   Matthew 16:16

a large gathering. I go over everything with the individual prior to the event.

The New Testament does not declare who can administer baptism. For children I encourage parents to do so, both mother and father if possible. For adults I encourage the person God used to lead him or her to Christ to do the baptism. Most people are comfortable having the minister do baptisms so I have done many. One thing I like to avoid, following the example of the Apostle Paul, is having people boast that they were baptized by me as if they were baptized into my name.[31]

Because we do baptism by total immersion, I also talk with the individuals beforehand about what to wear. It is especially important for women to wear something that does not become see through when wet. When I do a baptism I get wet too. I do not wear waders. I get into the water with the new Christian.

Ordination

You may find yourself involved in ordaining someone to ministry or missionary work, or as in our church, we ordain those who are called to serve as Elders or

Deacons. Except for the concept of *"laying on of hands"*[32] there are no formal instructions in the New Testament for ordaining. We developed a formula for ordination with variations for church officers and people going into full-time ministry of some sort.[33] By ordaining ministers and missionaries we were declaring that we have examined the individual and found him or her to be faithful and able to serve. This is a responsibility we took very seriously.

---

31 First Corinthians 1:14–15
32 Acts 6:6; 8:17, First Timothy 4:14
33 Appendix L includes examples.

Chapter Seven
Miscellaneous Issues

In this final chapter we will briefly discuss miscellaneous issues that you should prepare for. These are things I had to figure out for myself. These became what I taught to interns and people I mentored in ministry. Later, they always expressed how much they appreciated the teaching.

Pastoral Visitation

There are four kinds of pastoral visits. There was a time when pastors were expected to regularly visit in the homes of the church members, as much as once each year. When churches were small that was a reasonable expectation. You may be in such a context. As a church grows it becomes more and more difficult for "the pastor" to visit all the church members but it is still important for you to make personal contact with your church members. People want to feel that they have access to the leader of their church. I have an acquaintance who was a member of a very large church in Detroit. He shared his excitement that the Lead Pastor visited had a family in their neighborhood that week. Whether you are in a large or small church you may not manage to visit every family every year nevertheless, it is good to make that contact. Keep records of your visits if for no other reason than that you can deflect criticism when someone complains that you are never available to your people.

If you are going to visit the families of your church, realize that since most such visits happen in the evening it will take you away from your family so be judicious with your time. Perhaps your spouse will accompany you but probably not. Never visit someone of the opposite sex when you are alone. If it is a couple you are okay. If not you must take someone, your spouse, along. If you are not married or if your spouse does not want to go with you, *do not go*. Even if the visit is in preparation for a funeral, do not go the home of someone of the opposite sex alone. I cannot overstate the importance of this propriety.

Realize that private visits often lead to talking of confidential things. The rules of confidentiality apply. If you are paying a visit specifically to discuss a problem take another church leader with you.

I advise against "cold turkey" visits. People are busy. If the visit is inconvenient with the family they may resent your presence. Make arrangements beforehand so that it is a good time for them and you. They will appreciate your respectfulness. One more thing, you do not want to arrive at someone's house when he/she/they are involved in something that could be embarrassing or illegal.

Another kind of pastoral visit is the follow–up of visitors to your worship service. As your church grows and you attract more and more visitors you may not be able to visit everyone. In a small or midsize church you will find that most families appreciate a visit from the leader of the church. One family visited our church as well as several others churches when they moved to town, eventually joining our church and becoming important leaders. They told me we were the only church that visited in their home to welcome them.

If you don't have time to follow up with all the visitors, enlist the help of other staff and volunteer leaders.

A third kind of visit is evangelistic. Not many churches have specific programs for evangelistic calling but there are times when it is appropriate. It may be someone who is not a believer but who visited the church and asked to learn more about Christianity or your church specifically, or it may be someone a church member recommended that you visit. These can be tricky because the subject may not want you there. Assuming that he/she/they are interested to learn something about Christian faith, this is the work of an evangelist, you.

When I made an evangelistic visit I did not take a Bible along. I know what I should be sharing with them Biblically and I do not want them thinking, *"Well that's what your Bible says. Mine is different."* For that reason I always asked them for their Bible. If they did not have one (most people have one around somewhere) you probably know enough to guide them and can offer to provide a Bible for them later.

Finally you will make pastoral visits in hospitals or care facilities for church members or others. When you do, try to remember that to that patient and family, you represent Christ. Accept that sentiment. Your prayers are no more effective than their prayers, but they may feel like yours are. Be Jesus to them.

Interns

Most Bible colleges and seminaries require (or at the very least encourage) an internship for ministry students to learn from a seasoned pastor for a length of time before graduating. You may be called upon to lead an intern. For the sake of the student do not waste this opportunity. A poor or negative intern experience probably will do more harm than good.

Some schools have a planned curriculum for an internship, guiding the student and mentor through specific learning. Some trust you to provide that guidance. Much of what I have written in this book comes from my times working with interns or in mentoring relationships. Much of what is included in the appendices of this book is easily photocopied material I shared with students and mentees.

Have a plan if you are leading an intern. Choose the topics you wish someone had taught you and make your teaching time valuable. Spend a lot of time with the student. Suggest a few books to read and discuss. Choose books that are not taxing to read as the student is already being overwhelmed with information about the job of ministry. Some time–tested books I have used throughout my ministry are *Ordering Your Private World*[34] and *The Seven Laws of Teaching*.[35] Both are extremely valuable. I also suggest they read *How Do You Say "I Love You?"*[36], and *How To Really Love Your Child*.[37] Both of these will become valuable to the student some day when he or she is involved in a pastoral counseling relationship.

With about a month left in the internship ask the student if there is anything you have not covered that he or she wishes to learn. At the end of the internship do a debrief session with the student. Ask about what was helpful or what you could have done better. Share honestly with the student about areas you think he or she should work on.

If the school requires any paperwork from you, get it done in a timely manner while encouraging the student to do his or hers. I encourage you to follow up with the school to make sure everything that was required or expected has been completed. It is good for you to learn along with the student. Be prepared to write an honest reference when he or she is pursuing a ministry position.

---

34 MacDonald, *Ordering Your Private World*.

35 Gregory, *Seven Laws of Teaching*.

36 Swihart, *How do You Say "I Love You?"*

37 Campbell, *How To Really Love Your Child*.

Community Involvement

A pastor does well to be involved in his community. Social clubs, fraternities, volunteer service organizations, and sports teams are great opportunities for you to get to know your community outside your congregation. Serving on one or more boards of directors demonstrates your love for the people you live near. Opportunities to serve as chaplain to a hospital, fire department, or police department are also ways to be involved in your community.

Most communities have a ministers group that meets regularly. You may not see eye-to-eye theologically with every other minister but you can still fellowship and worship together. Unless someone is proclaiming heresy, learning how other ministers think about and do ministry will help you as you grow and learn in your ministry.

That said, be careful how much time is given to community activities. You will likely be criticized for *"spending too much time outside the church"*, especially if someone feels neglected or simply lonely. Remember you are already balancing your time between your church, your family, and yourself. Choose wisely.

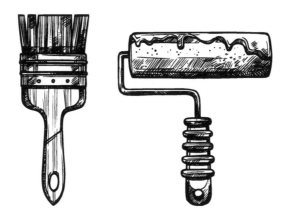

Afterward:

My Most Important Advice

If I could teach you nothing else I would want you to learn this. You will have your greatest success in ministry if you simply love your congregation. However profound your sermons, however well prepared your worship services, however charismatic or humorous you are personally, nothing will reach farther than your love, and nothing will stop you faster than failing to love. Your congregants will know if your love is genuine.

This is especially poignant if you are following a previous minister who was much loved. David served as king for 40 years. He enjoyed great success intermingled with some notable failures. The love of the people for David was immeasurable. After David, his son Solomon also served as king for 40 years in one of the most prosperous periods in Israel's history, called by many *"The Golden Age"* of Israel.

Imagine how hard that must have been for the people who had grown used to such success to accept a new king. Imagine how hard that must have been for the guy who succeeded David and Solomon.

The next king of Israel was Solomon's son Rehoboam. When he accepted the throne the people . . . *said to him: "Your father put a heavy yoke on us, but now lighten the harsh labor and the heavy yoke he put on us, and we will serve you."*[38] Notice, having enjoyed a great king and endured a not–so–great king, all they asked was that he treat them well. They showed him the respect of being their king.

When the people of Israel asked Rehoboam to treat them well he said to them, *"Go away for three days and then come back to me."*[39] Fair enough. Reheboam needed to decide what kind of king he would be. Some men have been known to turn down kingship because they didn't want the responsibilities or to deal with the expectations.

What did Rehoboam do? *"King Rehoboam consulted the elders who had served his father Solomon during his lifetime. 'How would you advise me to answer these people?' he asked. They replied, 'If today you will be a servant to these people and serve them and give them a favorable answer, they will always be your servants.'"*[40]

Those were wise men and their advice was sound. I offer you the same advice. Love and serve your congregation. Love your people and they will respect and follow you. They will support you when you succeed and build you up when you fail.

---

38 First Kings 12:3–4
39 First Kings 12:5
40 First Kings 12:6–7

Appendix A
Illustrations for Funeral Sermons[41]

Example One: For a person born between 1910 and about 1935

In 1998 Tom Brokaw published a book about the generation of Americans who grew up during the Great Depression with all of its hardships and deprivation.[42] In this book he coined the term *"The Greatest Generation"* to describe them. This generation beat the depression and sent millions of our countrymen to fight WW2 while those who stayed home produced the materiel necessary to execute that war. Those who survived the war built and rebuilt American industry, creating the greatest economy in the history of the world.

The stories that come from the people of this generation are a history lesson of what made America great: Families separated with children farmed out to relatives; collecting coal along the rail road tracks for heating and cooking; selling produce on the street corner; husbands and fathers taking any odd job that came along in order to provide; wives and mothers making a single item of clothing last far beyond it's normal time of wear and tear; families eating potatoes and more potatoes day after day, or not eating at all. I've heard the stories from my parents who were children of the depression.

It wasn't the hardships that made this a great country. It was the way this particular generation faced and defeated the hardships of economic depression and the evil of world war. They earned the title, *"The Greatest Generation"* because they were builders, not destroyers. They were loyal, faithful people who cared about country and other people first and themselves second.

---

41   In sermons and teaching I often used contractions (e.g. we're, that's, you'll) as taught by Professor Don Sunukjian
42   Brokaw, *Greatest Generation*.

According to Tom Brokaw, *". . . this is the greatest generation any society has produced"* because the men and women fought not for fame and recognition but because it was the right thing to do.

Jane Doe was one of that Greatest Generation and perfectly fits the description.

Example Two: For someone who was a child during The Great Depression

Let's think about what it means for someone to be 100 years old: Born after WW1 she saw automobiles go from a radical and novel idea that only the rich could afford to being an everyday expectation for every income level. She was an early teen when the Great Depression hit. She lived through WW2, the Korean War, the war in Viet Nam, the radical 60's, the turbulent 80's, Y2K, the first African American President, and in the last few years, the dividing of America by identity politics.

I want you to return to the Great Depression for a moment. Imagine being a middle school and high school girl in those days. I heard the stories from my parents who were children of the depression: families separated with children farmed out to relatives; collecting coal along the rail road tracks for heating and cooking; selling produce on the street corner; husbands and fathers taking any odd job that came along in order to provide; wives and mothers making a single item of clothing last far beyond it's normal time of wear and tear; families eating potatoes and more potatoes day after day, or not eating at all.

Imagine being a young girl trying to be pretty with little money for nice clothes and jewelry and make-up. Some of the women of my family who lived through that experience came out very bitter. As I read the things you wrote in Jane's 100th birthday celebration, I see a classy lady, who rather than becoming bitter, chose to enjoy life and become loving and unselfish. I see a woman who learned that life is better when you put others first.

Example three: For a Christian

The Parable of the Twins can serve as a good opening or closing of a funeral.[43] This can be found with a little research. I added my own touches each time I used it.

Example Four: Grief, the Price of Loving

When you lose one you love and who loves you it hurts. It's a pain that you cannot avoid nor can anyone take it away from you. There is no medicine or procedure that removes this part of life. You grieve. You grieve however you choose. There is no right or wrong way. There is only your way. There is also no time limit on grieving.

A wise woman in our church once shared with me that grief never ends. It changes. It fades with time but it doesn't completely go away. I hope your grief never goes away completely for that means you haven't stopped loving her.

Grief is not a sign of weakness nor is it to be unexpected. Grief is the price of love. If you didn't love Jane or if she didn't love you there would be no grief. Because you love and because she loves, you grieve at her passing. It's a small price to pay for having enjoyed her in your life.

Example Five: A tribute recognizing a life well lived (in contrast to sour, bitter people)[44]

The paradox of our time in history is that we have taller buildings but shorter tempers, wider freeways but narrower viewpoints. We spend more, but have less, we buy more, but enjoy less. We have bigger houses and

---

43   There are many different variations of this parable. Finding the original is next to impossible. I started with an iteration by Salesian Sisters re–writing parts of it for my purpose

44   This piece is attributed to George Carlin in tribute to his wife who did not settle for superficial living. The true source is highly debated. It is certainly consistent Carlin's style.

smaller families, more convenience, but less time. We have more degrees but less sense, more knowledge, but less judgment, more experts, yet more problems, more medicine, but less wellness.

We drink too much, smoke too much, spend too recklessly, laugh too little, drive too fast, get too angry, stay up too late, get up too tired, read too little, watch TV too much, and pray too seldom. We've learned how to make a living, but not a life. We've added years to life, but not life to years. We plan more but accomplish less. We've learned to rush but not to wait. We build more computers to hold more information, to produce more copies than ever, but we communicate less and less.

These are times of fast foods and slow digestion, big men and small character, steep profits and shallow relationships. These are the days of two incomes but more divorce, fancier houses, but broken homes. These are days of quick trips, disposable diapers, throwaway morality, one night stands, overweight bodies, and pills that do everything from cheer, to quiet, to kill.

Example Six: For a sudden and unexpected death

The late astronomer Carl Sagan, in his book Cosmos made the following statement, *"The size and age of the cosmos are beyond ordinary human understanding. Lost somewhere between immensity and eternity is our tiny planetary home. In a cosmic perspective, most human concerns seem insignificant, even petty."*[45]

With all due respect for Mr. Sagan, I disagree. I believe our human concerns are in fact very significant. I find no comfort in being told that my concerns are petty and insignificant. This is especially true when my concern is that my friend has died and his family is mourning. I think our human concerns are very important.

We didn't come here today to consider petty insignificant things. We came here because someone we love has died. We came to love and support this family by remembering and celebrating the life of Dick Doe. And that matters.

---

45   Sagan, *Cosmos.*

Example Seven: Another for an unexpected death

On January 3, 1999 NASA launched the Mars Polar Lander bound for the fourth planet. This $156 million machine, part of a $350 million project was intended to study the surface of Mars to see if life could exist there. Twelve minutes from touchdown on December 3 of that year NASA lost contact with the lander. It was determined that during its descent to the surface of the Red Planet a computer malfunction caused by deployment of its landing legs resulted in the engines shutting down allowing the craft to be destroyed on impact. Years of planning and preparing, eleven months of waiting, then disaster.

To the scientists who worked on this project it was like a punch in the gut. They had invested so much time and energy into this. They had thought of everything, except the effect the extension of the landing legs would have on the computers. No one anticipated such a catastrophic end. When you get word of a sudden death like Dick's, it's like a punch in the gut. No one knew he had a problem with his heart that would result in such a catastrophic end.

Example Eight: To illustrate that God accepts all who believe in Him

It seems to me that most people develop their own philosophy of life and expect to get to heaven based on their goodness. It doesn't work that way. We have to do it God's way. We can't be good enough. We have to accept Jesus Christ. When we do we become good enough through Him.

Stephen Brown was a wealthy man. Wealthy enough to purchase a Rolls Royce to travel around Europe. Not a bad car I suppose, however this one experienced a breakdown somewhere in France. Brown contacted the dealer from whom he purchased the car who then sent someone to repair his car. After several months and not having received a bill he contacted the dealer to settle up. They said, *"Rolls Royce has no record of any of their cars ever having a breakdown."* Of course some of their cars do break down from time to time. But when they fix it, they purge every record.

That's how it is with God. If we turn to Him, accept His truth, He keeps no record of our sins.

Example Nine: To encourage the family to enjoy stories about their loved one[46]

Lawyer and author Ed Hayes wrote a story called *The Little Tin Box*, about an old couple on the day their belongings were sold at auction. Having lost their farm, all of their lives' accumulations were sold off one piece at a time. After the long day was over and everyone had left, Tom and Mary were alone in their house with just a kitchen table and some chairs and an old bed upstairs. They were to be picked up in the morning.

They sat down at the table and placed the only thing they had left on it: a tin box that had almost sold but Tom rescued it. Mary was the first to speak, *"They almost sold your little tin box."* *"Yeah. That was close, wasn't it?"* Tom said as he slowly opened the lid of the box. To the average eye it appeared almost empty, but in reality it was filled almost to the top. The old battered tin box was filled with memories.

As the story goes Tom and Mary slowly took notes and small items out of the tin box. As they examined them, each reminded them of a happening or event long past: *This is the day you asked me to marry you; This is the day our first son was born; This is the time we travelled to Yellowstone Park and saw Old Faithful; This is the day our daughter was diagnosed with cancer.*

Nothing in the box had significant value in itself, but every piece brought back a memory of the love that they've shared and the things God brought them through.

---

46 Hayes, *Pair of Parables*.

Example Ten: Death, the Great Equalizer[47]

A bi-annual event that sports fans, especially golf fans, enjoy is The Ryder Cup, a contest between players from Europe and the United States. The 2008 Captain of the United States Ryder Cup team was Paul Azinger. In 1987 Azinger was named the PGA Player of the Year. By age thirty–three he had won ten tournaments including the PGA Championship. Then he was diagnosed with cancer. He later wrote how fear overwhelmed him that he could die from this illness. Then a different reality struck, that he was going to die anyway, whether from cancer or something else. It's just a question of when.

Facing the possibility of his own death he remembered the chaplain to pro golfers, Larry Moody, saying, *"We're not in the land of the living going to the land of the dying. We're in the land of the dying going to the land of the living."*

Paul Azinger beat cancer and returned to golfing. He later shared that even though he won a lot of money playing golf having won a lot of professional tournaments (sixteen), the happiness they brought was only temporary. Real joy and contentment he found in a personal relationship with Jesus Christ. He still faced problems and difficulties in life but, making a clever golf analogy, in Jesus he found the answer to the six foot hole.

You know, it doesn't matter what our lives are all about, death is the great equalizer. God has taken Dick Doe home, and according to the Bible, he now has a new body with no cancer or illness. He's probably right now standing with a choir of angels singing and enjoying the sounds of praise.

---

47 This can be used especially for someone who died from cancer or another lethal illness.

Example Eleven: For a victim of murder

We're here today because there is evil in the world. I recently completed a study of the Book of Revelation in my sermons at our church. I tried to uncover the mystery of a book that confuses many people, by teaching this simple message. God, who created everything, including spiritual beings like angels as well as humans, desires that we live eternally with Him in heaven. He gave his created beings the free will to choose to love Him or ignore Him. One such spiritual being, known as Satan, chose not only to ignore God but to try to become God. The result is a battle between God's forces of good and Satan's forces of evil. That's why there is evil in the world.

In the end God will win, but until then, evil touches us in many ways. Perhaps the worst is when one evil person hurts a good person. We're here today because evil took life from a wonderful Christian woman. We're terribly saddened, and we're angry, but we will not let evil take away our love for Jane or her love for us. We will grieve. We will cry. We will experience bouts of loneliness. We will miss her. We will also celebrate for her because she is now free and at peace in the presence of Jesus.

Appendix B
Samples of Funerals[48]

Example One: For a family grieving a loss but celebrating a loved one's transition to eternal life

Play: *"I Can Only Imagine"*[49]

That beautiful song makes us think about what happens after we die if we're called to Heaven. What will it be like? What will we see? What will we do? Today is a good time to think about that because we acknowledge today that Jane Doe is there now.

Incongruence

Incongruence is a condition of being inconsistent, not appropriate, or not harmonious. Incongruence is the basis of most humor. The comedian identifies a situation and then points out something that doesn't fit and perhaps we hadn't noticed. That makes us laugh. Here's a silly example. Our church is involved in a ministry called *"Free the Girls"*. The women of our church donate new or gently used bras which are shipped to locations in third world countries where they're given to a mission. The women of the mission then sell the bras and that's how they make a living. Now, here's an incongruence: We have a sign in the church telling ladies where to leave the bras. It simply says, *"Bra Drop-Off Location."* Now when you see a sign in a church that says *"Bra Drop-off Location"* you begin to wonder what's going on at that church.

---

48 These are not the complete services, but enough to give you an idea of how you can proceed.

49 Mercy Me, *I Can Only Imagine*, 1999.

Incongruence describes a celebration of life event. It's a sad time, a time of grieving and crying. It's also a time of rejoicing a life well lived. We grieve because someone we love and who loves us has died, but we choose to celebrate because of all that she means to us and we know that a week ago Jesus said to her, *"Well done my child. Come home!"* There's going to be crying today and for a while. It's OK. Tears of grief are cathartic. They help us cope with tragedy and loss. We grieve when someone we love dies.

I want you to understand, grief is your last act of love for Jane. In your grief you express your love. You grieve because your mother is gone; because your grandmother is no longer available to love on you; because your sister can't call you up just to talk; because your friend isn't around to share a laugh. You grieve because this is very personal. Grief is yours. However and for however long it's your grief. No one should tell you what it should look like. Know this, while it is OK to grieve, you don't need to grieve for Jane. She's home. Jane sat where you now sit at least six times, mourning the loss of a loved one. She will never cry again. There are no tears in Heaven. There God will wipe away every tear. There will be no more death, no more mourning, no more crying, and no more pain.[50] So let the celebration begin. Let's share some thoughts and stories about Jane.

One special thing about Jane that we celebrate today is that she loved Jesus. For years she worked most or all Sundays, but after retiring she loved to worship. Going to church was not a *"have to"* thing. She went to church because she wanted to. She loved the Lord.

Something I've never told you before, at each of the five previous funerals I've shared with your family, she always encouraged me to share the Gospel. She wanted you to know Jesus. She'll come back and haunt me if I don't tell you that she wants you to enjoy this same salvation she's now experiencing.

---

50   Revelation 7:17, 21:4

She wants you to know that God loves you and wants your company for eternity. He wants to share the glory and beauty of Heaven with you. He wants to share a love relationship with you. God's love and salvation are available to anyone who chooses to believe and love Jesus. *"To all who received Him, to those who believed in His name, He gave the right to become children of God."*[51]

It doesn't matter who you are or what you've done, you may choose Jesus. No one is so bad that God can't love you. And no one is so good that you don't need God's love. Jesus said anyone who chooses may come to Him, but you must choose. In fact, God's salvation is available only to those who choose to believe and love Jesus. *"Salvation is found in no one else, for there is no other name under heaven given to men by which we must be saved."*[52] God loves you so much He chose to pay for your sins by being crucified in a brutal execution on an ugly cross.

We wear a cross as jewelry on a necklace or bracelet, or we decorate our homes with a cross. That's OK, but understand, the cross was not a charm. It was a very cruel instrument of torture and death. Jesus suffered on a cross so that when we die, we can experience all the beauty and peace and love on Heaven.

Jane believes and loves Jesus. Today she's experiencing Heaven in a way that we can only imagine. That's why we celebrate even while we grieve. One day every one of us will lie in a coffin just like this. When it's your turn, will this be your final destiny?

God will never force Himself on you. In His grace He allows you to choose. Will you choose Jesus or the world? If you're not sure that you're destined for Heaven, or if you don't understand what this is all about, please talk to me. As long as you're thinking about it, don't let the day slip away until you are certain of salvation, because one day your opportunity to choose will be over.

---

51 John 1:12
52 Acts 4:12

In 2008 a Christian singer/song writer Mandisa met a woman who was pregnant with a boy she would name Andrew. Andrew was stillborn. Mandisa wanted to bless his mother Rebecca so she wrote a song from Andrew's perspective called *You Wouldn't Cry*.[53] It was all about the wonders the little boy was experiencing in Heaven with God. Rebecca said it brought her comfort to know that when she sees her son again he's going to show her around Heaven and all the things he's been experiencing.

Jane would sing that song for you today if she could. She would have you know that what she's now experiencing is far greater, more beautiful, more comforting, and more joyful than anything we can ever know on earth. Please enjoy this song and receive it as Jane's final message to you.

Play: *You Wouldn't Cry*

---

53   Mandisa, *You Wouldn't Cry*, 2009

Example Two: For the tragic death of a young person who has accepted Christ, however had strayed from the faithful living

Prayer

Thank you for giving some of your time to share your love with Mandy's family this evening. This is not our typical Thursday evening activity. Sometimes it's important for us to set aside our priorities for the sake of friends and family. Tonight is one of those nights. We're here to encourage and bless Mandy's family.

I don't know Mandy. I know her mom. I can't really speak much about her. I read her obituary and met with Miranda and Kathy so I know a little bit about her, but unfortunately I can't share common experiences. I've learned that Mandy was an artistic girl. She had a talent for writing, able to put her thoughts on paper in a way that made sense to a reader. She loved her family. She was selective of friends. She liked animals. She enjoyed the simplicity of having fun and liked to make others laugh. Most importantly she accepted Jesus Christ as Savior and was baptized in 2015 along with Miranda and Kathy. For that we are comforted to know she is saved for eternity.

I realize that her recently troubled life seems incongruent with her belief in Jesus, nor does her extreme sadness seem consistent with that faith. If you will give me a few minutes of your time I hope to offer you comfort concerning Mandy. Her death is certainly tragic. Who could have predicted, who could have imagined that her life on Earth would end so suddenly and mysteriously?

Of course we know the cause of death but we don't know how it transpired. We may never know. We know that this fun–loving girl with the world before her and with honest faith in Christ somehow fell into troubled despair that ended in this tragic way. I want you to understand an uncomfortable truth: *"Our enemy, the Devil, prowls around like a lion looking for someone to devour."*[54] He has one goal, to

---

54   First Peter 5:8

destroy. He sought to destroy the relationship between Mandy and Jesus.

Satan thinks that by interrupting her walk with Christ he will keep her from eternity in heaven. She's not the first and won't be the last child of God to be dragged away by him.

- A man named Job, famous for his patience fell to such despair that he lamented even being born.[55]

- Elijah, a prophet of God actually asked God to take his life ". . . *I have had enough, Lord, take my life,"*[56] he said.

- King David, known as *"a man after God's own heart"* struggled because his life was so messed up.

- The Apostle Paul, the guy who wrote most of the New Testament, at one point despaired of life.

Satan thought that he could create separation between Mandy and Jesus. He thought that if he could trouble her spirit she would be kept far from God and away from eternal life with him.

Many people think that way because they misunderstand the love of God. In what is probably the most well–known sentence in the Bible Jesus said, *"God loved the world so much that He gave His only Son so that whoever believes in Him will not perish but have eternal life."*[57] God is way ahead of Satan. His love is greater than all of our sin, it reaches deeper than our despair, it is stronger than our weaknesses, and is more enduring than our doubt.

Satan may win some individual battles but he has not and will not win the war. Mandy, based on her faith in Jesus is promised eternal life. The Gospel is not, *"God loved the world so much that He gave His only Son so that whoever lives a sinless life will be saved."* It's not, *"God loved the world so much that He gave His only Son so that whoever experiences complete happiness on Earth will be saved."* It's not, *"God*

---

55 Job 3:3–26
56 First Kings 19:4b
57 John 3:16

loved the world so much that He gave His only Son so that whoever defeats the devil will be saved." The Gospel is that *"God loved the world so much that He gave His only Son so that whoever believes in Him will be saved."*

Notice two important truths in this Gospel. First, there is nothing anyone can do to earn eternal life. It is by grace through faith that we can be saved. No one is saved because he or she does the right stuff. If we live righteous lives it's because we are saved, not *in order* to be saved.

The opposite is also true, no one is lost for eternity by what they do. Behavior reflects what we believe. Sometimes it's the result of getting messed up temporarily, but that doesn't determine our destiny. Jesus did what was necessary to assure us that not even sin can separate us from the love of God. We trust Him and because we love Him, we try to live in a Christ–like way. This is not to say that our behavior doesn't matter. It does. It matters because our behavior shows that we love God.

If Mandy's behavior was not Christ–like it doesn't mean she was lost. It means she was troubled. God's love is greater than our troubles.

The second truth we find in this Gospel is that God gives us the free will to choose Him or deny Him. We each choose our destiny. If He wanted to, God could control every aspect of our lives, that way we would never sin. But then, it wouldn't be because we love Him. So He allows us to choose for ourselves. Mandy chose to believe God and trust His love to be greater than her troubles.

We are each given that same choice; we can believe in Jesus or we can deny Him. The choice you make will determine your destiny. If you choose to believe Him you will know with confidence that Mandy is not lost. Jesus knows exactly where she is.

Jesus said, *"Do not let your hearts be troubled. Trust in God; trust also in me. In my Father's house are many rooms; if it were not so, I would have told you. I am going there to prepare a place for you. And if I go and prepare a place for you, I will come back and take you to be with me that you also may be where I am"*[58]

You grieve her passing. Grief is the price of love. You grieve because you love her. If you didn't love her, there would be no grief.

You grieve her passing but know that she is now in the hands of God. There is no better or safer place to be.

Prayer

---

58   John 14:1–3

Example Three: For an older person.

Remember the Good Times

I read a story, probably fictitious, about three older women sitting around a kitchen table, enjoying some coffee and catching up on things; kids, grandchildren, ailments, etc. One of the women got a serious look on her face and said, *"I'm getting concerned. I think I'm losing memory. The other day I was standing at the bottom of the stairs holding an armful of clothes and couldn't remember if I was taking them to the laundry, or preparing to fold and put them away."*

"I know what you mean," said another of the women. *"The other day I was standing at the refrigerator holding a jar of mayonnaise, but suddenly my mind went blank. I couldn't remember if I just took it out to spread it on a sandwich or was I putting it away."* The third woman looked at her friends with a bit of a smug smile and said, *"I'm sure glad I don't have to worry about that yet, knock on wood."* After a short pause she asked, *"Is somebody going to answer the door?"*

That story is good for a laugh, but there's a point to it. It seems that most people experience issues with memory as we age. Jane was spared that ignominy. She kept her faculties up to at least the last week of her life.

There's a simple saying that the family can tell you that exemplifies her life. Four words that describe the drive that carried Jane past the troubles of life: *"Remember the good times"*.

You see Jane had some challenges concerning which many people would have viewed life as completely bad, or at least not very good. But she managed to overcome so to enjoy the good times. Some would say that growing up with five brothers is enough to make life a bad thing. Jane became the *"princess."* I don't know if that's a testament to her or to her brothers, but it's one of the good things she remembered.

The first time I met Jane I noticed that she had tremors and thought she had Parkinson's or some similar ailment. I don't know what caused the tremors, I've never asked since it's none of my business, but I know that they didn't stop her from participating in the things she enjoyed, things that made life good. She loved working with handicapped adults. One could have expected her to consider herself handicapped. But Jane wouldn't give in to that. Instead she overcame and became a blessing to others.

Jane loved many good things in life like tending her flowers, or poking around the antique shops, or the Goodwill store where real treasures are waiting to be found. She loved animals, especially her dog and cat. She made a real connection with animals. More than anything she loved her family. I'm sure you have many anecdotes you could share about your relationship with her. Nate shared the other day about the good times on the pontoon boat and having lunch on the lake. Those are good memories and I encourage you to keep them fresh.

After we're finished here we're going to go to our other building for a dinner where I want you to tell fun stories. All you have to do is start talking about something she did or said and others will remember and laugh with you and add more thoughts and soon you'll all be remembering the good times with your mother, your aunt, your grandmother, your friend. And if tears slip in along the way, it's OK. They are good tears.

Don't ever forget how much you love her and how much she loved you. You'll get over the painful part of grieving one day, but don't get over the grief itself. You grieve because someone you love has passed on to eternal life. You defeat the pain when you remember the good times.

People who don't know Jesus tend to struggle with death on earth because it seems that this is the end. There's nothing good after this life. But for whoever will accept Jesus as Savior, there is something wonderful after this life, eternal life in Heaven. God loves us so much that He chose to live a life on earth in the person of Jesus and even to die in this life in order to secure salvation for us.

We had a guest preacher at our church last Sunday who reminded us that we don't have to be good enough to enjoy this promised eternal life. We don't have to be able to say all the right things. We don't have to do all the right things. We can be failures. We can stumble. We can have tremors. None of that matters. What matters is that we trust Jesus who forgives our sins.

I didn't know for sure if Jane was a believer but Mary Ann assured me that she was. So I say with confidence, while we may miss her, we don't have to worry about her eternal destiny. Jesus took care of that.

I know most of you here tonight, but I don't necessarily know where you are in your relationship with Jesus. I hope you have chosen to accept Him as your Savior. I remind you that that's a choice you have to make for yourself. No one can make that one for you. If you're not sure I invite you to come talk to me. I would love to tell you about Jesus' love.

Jane Doe is a kind sweet woman. That's what she takes to heaven. She loves her family. You love her. If you need to cry, you go ahead. Tears are amazingly cathartic. You grieve however and for however long you need to. But don't grieve like those who have no hope of eternal life. Keep in mind God's promise.

The Bible tells us that one day Jesus is coming back. Here is God's promise for that day: *"We will not all sleep, but we will all be changed, in a flash, in the twinkling of an eye, at the last trumpet. For the trumpet will sound, the dead will rise up and out of their graves, beyond the reach of death. At the same moment and in the same way, we'll all be changed."*[59]

Yes it sounds rather mysterious, but it's God's promise. And God keeps every promise.

Finally, once again I say, *"Remember the good times"*, and be encouraged, for Jane is not dead. She has changed from life on earth to life eternal.

---

59 First Corinthians 15:51–52

Example Four: For the mother of a friend. I did not know her personally nor did I know most of those attending the funeral.

Play: *On Eagle's Wings*[60]

Good afternoon. Thank you for being here this day. Your presence encourages and supports this family as they go through the loss of someone they love. That you would give up some of your afternoon tells them that you care. We're here to say *"Good–bye"* to Jane Doe, wife of the late Jim Doe and mother of Stan, Rob, Hugh, Tim, and Julie. She is grandmother to seven, great–grandmother to six, and aunt to many. She is a friend to many more, especially members of the VFW here in La Porte.

I'm not going to read her entire obituary. You can read it and you probably know it better than I. We have two purposes today. One is to celebrate her life and the other is to grieve with her family. We're going to talk about her, telling some stories and remembrances. Most of you know her far better than I so at this time we'll offer if anyone here would like to share your thoughts about Jane, we invite you to do so. You may stand where you are or if you'd rather you may use this podium.

Play: *When I Get Where I'm Going*[61]

A Noble Woman

I have entitled my message to you today, *A Noble Woman*. Ninety–five years old. Born in 1924 means she experienced her teen years during the Great Depression, called that not because it was a great time but because it was so vast, affecting every segment of American society. The very wealthy were, of course, less affected

---

60 Joncas, *On Eagle's Wings.*
61 Paisley, *When I Get Where I'm Going.*

than the rest of the country, but hardships were many for middle class and the poor.

I don't know Jane and I don't know what her early life was like, but I'm pretty sure she didn't come from wealth. There are not and were not many very wealthy families living in Westville, Indiana. She probably experienced the kinds of things my mother, who is about the same age, told me about those days. She probably never owned three pairs of blue jeans. Chances are she was lucky to have one. I doubt she had a closet full of dresses. She probably only needed one hanger. A teen girl during the depression didn't need a suitcase just for her make–up. How could she feel pretty? Standards of beauty were different then than now, but still, every girls wants to be pretty. She probably didn't get to travel the world and experience new things.

When you think about how much of a person's self–esteem and personality are affected by her possessions and opportunities, it's a wonder any kid made it out of that era with a sense of personal worth. How Jane survived those difficult years affected how she lived the rest of her life. She definitely didn't want you to suffer the same disappointments that she experienced.

My Webster's Dictionary describes the word "noble" in two ways. It refers to a person of a wealthy or aristocratic family, or one of exalted rank. In another context it refers to a person with out-standing positive qualities. Jane would not be considered a noble person of the first description. But what about outstanding positive qualities?

When I met with you last week you had many good things to say about her even while you expressed a troubled relationship at times. One thing that stood out to me, something that made sense to me, was that she did the best she could with what she had been given.

What tools did she have to work with? She wasn't rich. Her marriage wasn't what dreams are made of. She didn't have what we would call a happy life. When you consider her early life coupled with a troubled marriage, it's remarkable that she was able to provide you with a sense of normalcy. Raising four sons and a daughter each of whom is successful in life, she must have had some outstanding qualities. She did her best to make sure you knew that she loved you very much.

Sometimes she frustrated you as she tried to guide you to excellence. She had high standards and expected you to achieve. Frustration came when she let you know you didn't. Still she was very proud of each of you. She did her best to express personal strength. She wasn't afraid to stand on what she believed was right and resisted changing her mind. That can be either good or bad. She believed in herself and didn't want anyone speaking for her.

She was a generous woman. She did her best with her heart and money to support many different charities. She generously quit working when she felt the need to stay home and care for her ailing father. She wasn't afraid of work. She did her best to help provide for the family, holding down full–time jobs as well as giving a lot of time serving the VFW. She was a smart woman. Although not educated beyond high school she was a voracious reader, sometimes reading by firelight, sometimes reading far into the night. Her imagination came alive when she read, taking her to another world, different and probably more enjoyable than what she lived.

Jane did her best to be a fun mother. She read to you as you were growing. You remember the Childcraft Books. She read these to help you enjoy learning. Obviously she knew the value of education. You remember her entertaining you with monologues in which she became different characters, bringing them to life for you. You remember her reading spooky stories to you, then sending you off to bed. You remember playing a game in which you would draw a picture on her back with your finger and she tried to figure out what it was. If she got it wrong you erased it and tried again. Only later did you come to realize that she got a pleasant back scratching out of it. (I'm going to have to try that with my grandson.) You remember her preparing dough and mixing sauce from scratch to make pizza at home.

You remember her allowing a basset hound into the house. It was a concession, not because she liked dogs. Named Moses after the basketball player Moses Malone, he lost his welcome when he chewed up her glasses. He didn't last long. You remember how she loved music and dancing, and playing cards. You remember her helping you with Boy Scouts.

You remember how she did the grandma thing babysitting grandchildren, like Randy and later Troy. She looked for fun things to do with the little ones. She bought small things for Troy for which he gave her an IOU. The refrigerator was papered with them. She took him to Walmart to buy a fishing lure and he came home with a tackle box. Such is a woman who did her best for her family.

Sometimes you struggled in your relationship with your mother. Remember what she had to overcome to get along in the world. Was she a noble woman? She did her best with what she was given. Could she have done better? Maybe. Maybe not. But when you think of all of the good she did for you, maybe you can forgive her faults and say, *"Thank you God that I had a mother who loved me"*.

As I said earlier I don't know Jane. I know Jari and I've spoken with Rob. In the process I've learned some interesting things about her. I learned that she developed a love to travel; to see and experience new things, a love that she hoped to instill in you. I learned that she liked to watch political stuff on TV. I didn't ask what her affiliations are because I was told that she'd argue with you if you weren't on the same page. I learned that Julie was a bad influence on her, getting her to sneak out of Settlers Place (a care facility in which she lived her later life) late at night to go to Dairy Queen or McDonald's. It's not that it wasn't allowed but it felt like they were breaking curfew. That was fun.

I asked about her spiritual life. None of us knows exactly where she was spiritually. I learned she had some experiences with the

Christian religion. Did she come to know the Savior? None of us can say. She visited our church a few times and seemed to like what we were all about, and our style. She specifically asked for me to lead this funeral service, which I accepted as an honor. Jari told me that based on various experiences with her, she believes Jane was at peace spiritually.

If Jane was looking for truth, Jesus would have made Himself known to her. He wants people to know Him and trust Him in life and especially in death. His whole purpose for becoming a man was to offer Himself as a sacrifice to pay for our sins so that we can have a relationship with God.

Jesus said that He is like a shepherd who had a flock of one-hundred sheep. As he tucked them all safely away in the sheep pen one night he noticed one was missing. He left the ninety–nine safe sheep to go looking for that one lost lamb. That was risky because something could happen to the 99 while he was out searching. He trusted the 99 to care for each other. Because he loved the one lost sheep so much he bravely went looking for it.

If she was looking for Jesus, I'm confident that she found Him. Any person who honestly goes looking for Jesus will find Him. We find Him not because Jesus is lost but because He wants us to find and know Him. Jesus said, *"Ask and it will be given to you; seek and you will find; knock and the door will be opened to you. For everyone who asks receives; he who seeks finds; and to him who knocks, the door will be opened."*[62]

God will never refuse someone who honestly seeks Him. And so God doesn't demand a specific method of seeking. He doesn't require that everyone find Him through the same channel. Some people find Him at a stadium revival service, like Billy Graham used to do. Some find Him in the midst of crisis. Some find Him through involvement with a church. Some find Him in the solitude of their own minds and hearts.

---

62   Matthew 7:7–8

We must never judge another's relationship with God. There's reason to believe that Jane found what she was looking for somewhere in the recesses of her heart, and with that thought we say *"Good–bye mother. Good–bye aunt. Good–bye friend. May God welcome you into eternal life."* We can't know exactly what Heaven will be like. We're told it is a place of indescribable beauty with no evil, no tears, no sorry, and no pain.

I'd like to think that somewhere in God's awesome grace, He welcomed Jane home. In your mind, picture her entering heaven. What will it be like? I can only imagine.

Play: *I Can Only Imagine*[63]

---

63 Mercy Me, *I Can Only Imagine.*

Example Five: For a fallen Police Officer.

Welcome and thank you.

In 1998 Tom Brokaw published a book about the generation of Americans who came of age during the Great Depression with all of its hardships and deprivation.[64] Dick Doe was one of that Greatest Generation.

We're here today for three purposes. First, we're here to share in the grief of this dear family who lost their father, grand-father, uncle, and friend. We have come to shoulder some of the burden of grief. As we love on you perhaps we can lessen the hurt.

Second, we're here because an important member of our community has died. The first responders of La Porte County, the La Porte County Sherriff's Department, the La Porte City Police Department, the La Porte County Emergency Medical Services, and the citizens of La Porte have lost one of our own. It is a significant loss.

Third, we're here to honor and pay tribute to a man who spent his life serving and protecting our country, our county, and our city. Dick Doe is twice a hero. He is a hero who put his life on the line in World War 2. As part of the Signal Corps of the United States Army he was one of the war fighters who went ashore at Omaha Beach in the invasion of Normandy. He served in both the European and Pacific theaters of war earning many distinctions, medals, and ribbons. He is also a hero who put his life on the line every day for 25 years as an officer with the La Porte County Sherriff's Department. Dick willingly accepted the risk in order to serve and protect the citizens of our county. He chased fleeing suspects and once braved the blast of a shotgun through a door when arresting a dangerous man. He easily could have ignored the risks, but that's not what a good cop does.

---

64   This illustration can be found in Appendix A

One of the men who served alongside Dick for many years is going to share some things about him, the former Sheriff.

Sheriff speaks.

Having spent fourteen years as chaplain with the La Porte City Police Department I have a special place in my heart for this profession. We're all certainly aware of the animus toward police in our country today. In reality, it has always been like this for cops. In honor of Dick I offer this tribute:

Cops are people, just like us. Some are men, some are women. Some are young, some are old. Some are large, some are small. They come from all races and economic classes, from all religions and backgrounds.

Cops do things most of us don't want to think about. They deliver a baby one day and the next hold the hand of a dying accident victim. One day they return stolen goods to someone whose home was burgled and the next they tell a family that their loved one has died. Many nights they go to sleep wondering why they chose such a crummy job.

People sarcastically ask, *"Where's a cop when you need one?"* then when they get pulled over for speeding complain, *"Why don't you go find real criminals?"*

Cops are criticized for not solving crimes in one hour like they do on TV, when in real life what they get from the public is, *"I didn't see nothin'."* They're criticized for not finding a lost little boy among half a million people when the only information they receive is, *"He's about this tall with blond hair."*

When cops make an arrest they're *"picking on me"* but when they give someone a break they're *"not doing their job."* If he's a good cop well, *"that's what he's getting paid for."* If he makes a mistake *"he's a lousy cop just like the rest of them."* When he stops a thug it's *"police* brutality." When he's not at the scene of a crime it's because *"he's somewhere eating donuts."*

In his career a cop will see a life time of misery, bloodshed, and grieving families. He'll witness broken families and domestic violence, abused children and neglected pets. Cops are mistreated, disrespected, and assaulted by the same people for whom they risk their lives. When they hold the line on crime they're reminded, *"I pay your salary."*

Sometimes cops receive medals or letters of commendation, but generally after helping a citizen in distress they're satisfied with an occasional hand shake or hug and a *"God bless you, son."*

Dick Doe was the kind of man I want wearing the uniform. It is my distinct honor to speak about him this morning. Whenever you encounter a cop remember, he's just like Dick. His family wants him to come home. He deserves our respect.

There is much more to Dick Doe than a soldier and a cop. He was a loving family man who enjoyed adventure. Dick was sort of a self–taught pilot. He could fly just about anything. He liked to scare the people riding in the plane with him, pretending to have engine failure or making nose dives and sharp turns. He once ran out of gas because he forgot to switch fuel tanks when the first one went low. He landed in a crop field but managed to get the craft air borne again.

He and some friends once rode all the way to Texas in a rumble seat to buy a horse (some of you are too young to know what a rumble seat is). They didn't buy the horse. He loved fishing but apparently Amanda could outfish him. On one occasion it was Dick zero, Amanda four.

For most of the ninety–five years he walked this earth he was a kind, generous, strong–willed, and humorous man. He had a quiet but polite wit. He never intended to hurt anyone but wasn't afraid to if necessary.

He worked a number of jobs throughout his life including owning a grocery store and a riding stable. He sold pots and pans door to door. An interesting thing, his was the first house in Hanna to get gas service from NIPSCO. He forcefully adopted a cat, Rudy, from Candy's house. I say forcefully because that wasn't the plan, but he just fell in love with that cat and took him when he went home. Dick knew what he liked and wanted and didn't mind telling you if you got it wrong, like cooking his grits too long.

Over the last several years, as Dick needed more and more care a lot of people stepped up and helped with the responsibilities. In this you showed your love.

On Benny's behalf I want to acknowledge and thank certain people: American Legion; VFW; Sheriff Jim Byrd; Great Lakes Hospice; CAN; Cam & Donna Bower; Trevor and Diane Wentz; Doug and Betty Long; Candy; Carl and Amanda; The Rogers, Jackson and Karen and Rachel and Irene and Trey. Most of all, Tammy. You gave selflessly of yourself, treating Dick as the most important person in the world. Finally, Benny our friendship started at the YMCA playing basketball nearly 40 years ago and has grown significantly from there. I am honored that you and Tammy allowed me to lead your wedding eighteen years ago.

You are faithful members of our church and you are truly loving servant–hearted Christians. It's your faith in Jesus that gives you courage right now. You know that death on earth is not the end of life but the beginning of new life. While you'll miss him greatly you know that he lives and you too will experience resurrection one day.

Benny and Tammy, I know that sometimes Dick could get your goat, but you love him. You're going to grieve. Your grief will be tempered by the knowledge of eternal life in Heaven. Understand, grief is the price of love. If you didn't love him there'd be no grief at all.

All of us here want you to know, whenever you need someone to talk to or a shoulder to cry on, we're here. We love you and will do whatever we can for you. May God bless you all as you say "Good–bye" to Dick Doe.

Example Six: For the oldest member of our church, who happened to be a "die–hard" Cubs fan.[65]

Prayer

Video – *Take Me Out to the Ball Game* sung by Harry Carey at a Cubs game.

Video – *Final out of 2016 World Series*

Joyful Sadness

It felt like it was never going to happen. We were prepared to be disappointed. Things have a way of going wrong even with the best of intentions and efforts. We could only watch as things fell apart but it was nothing new to us. We were used to it. Nobody suffers like Cubs fans. But this time it was different. After giving up 5–1 and 6–3 leads, our faltering Cubbies got a reprieve when rain halted game seven of the 2016 World Series for seventeen minutes.

Momentum shifted and after scoring the go–ahead run in the top of the tenth inning, our guys held off the challenging Indians for an 8–7 victory to win the World Series for the first time in 108 years. On that November night everything was right in the world.

It felt like it was never going to happen. We were used to seeing Thelma come into our sanctuary on the arm of Craig or Barbara or almost anyone who was available to assist her. She sat right over there, on the aisle so she could see forward when people were standing to sing. She was here every Sunday until her health slowed her down. It was difficult for her to go around greeting people but just about everyone found their way to her. Sandra was everybody's aunt or grandma and we all wanted a hug. Then her health turned and she couldn't get out every week. Soon she was living at Miller's Health and Rehab Facility. She was tired and while she was thankful

---

65 She lived long enough to see her Cubbies win a World Series. This demonstrates how you can use special circumstances in a funeral.

to be alive, she was ready to go on to eternal life. Sandra knew she would go into the hands of Jesus.

On the Sunday before Christmas we got word that she had gone home. We're saddened because we've lost our small package of love, but we're thrilled for Sandra. It is a joyful sadness. We knew that everything was right in the world. We're here today not to mourn, although we will, but to celebrate a wonderful woman. She was a model of motherhood, a loving aunt and grandmother, a great friend, and a lovely example of a Christian. She will be missed and we will shed many tears, none–the–less our intention is to rejoice with her for she has received the prize for which she lived.

From the first time Sandra came to our church to worship we fell in love with her. She was a classy lady. She loved all of us equally. I was her favorite, at least I tell myself that. Not only did Sandra love everyone, everyone loved Sandra. She enjoyed the love. That's one of the things that kept her spirits up. The power of Christian fellowship, although it can't be quantified, is one of the strongest forces on earth.

I loved visiting her, laughing and sharing. She was the keenest ninety–six year old I've ever known. Her mind was as sharp as ever. When you went to her house she always had a dish of Hershey's Minis for you to select from. Of course we talked about the Cubs and our plans for Carl and me to walk her around the bases at Wrigley Field when she turned a century old. She said she should probably also have her doctor along. I said, *"Hey! I'm a doctor!"* I think she meant she wanted her physician not a Doctor of Ministry.

We talked about our love for the Lord and how good He has been to us. We talked about some of you. Rest assured she never said a bad word about anybody. She accepted everyone and har-bored not a judgmental bone in her body.

We talked about the people who regularly visited with her: Jen Brown came often and did little things for her. She was the bath lady. Lana Murphy would come over to make sure her hair was pretty.

She had her own personal mailman, Marvin Cline, who watched over her. Barbara and Craig especially looked after her so she didn't have to live in a nursing home. Jon and Darlene, you sacrificed so much to be here with her over the last few years. You are a special blessing. She knew that all of you and others were God's gift.

We talked about how she was a "Rosie the Riveter". During WW2 many women worked in the factories producing the materiel necessary to prosecute that war. Connie Reynolds, who we said "Good–bye" to two weeks ago, worked in a factory making boots for the soldiers. Sandra was a riveter. I don't remember what war machines she worked on but she was proud to do her part to support our fighting men.

Every Sunday and every visit she told me she loved me. Before my emotions get to me I'm going to ask several people to share some prepared comments in a sort of tag–team eulogy.

Eulogies

Sandra would be disappointed with me if I did not talk about the faith she lived. Sandra knew that Jesus is the Christ, the Son of the Living God. She loved to worship and loved to talk about Jesus. Faith in Jesus was an important part of our relationship and our talks and it was important to Sandra that people would see Jesus in her. That's why I know she would want me to present the Gospel message.

I'm going to tell you two golf stories to share two things about the Gospel that I want you to think about. The first is about a professional golfer from about seventy years ago named Tommy Bolt. He was a brash man known as Thunder Tommy. He was playing in Los Angeles with a caddy who had a reputation of constant chatter. Before they teed off, Bolt told him, *"Don't say a word to me. And if I ask you something, just answer yes or no."*

During the round, Bolt found the ball next to a tree, where he had to hit under a branch, over a lake and onto the green. He got down on his knees and looked through the trees and sized up the shot. *"What do you think?"* he asked the caddy. *"Five iron?"* *"No, Mr. Bolt,"* the caddy said. *"What do you mean, not a five iron?"* Bolt snorted. *"Watch this shot."* The caddy just rolled his eyes.

Bolt hit the shot. The ball missed the branch, cleared the lake and stopped about two feet from the hole. He turned to his caddy, handed him the five iron and said, *"Now what do you think about that? You can talk now."* *"Mr. Bolt,"* the caddy said, *"that wasn't your ball."*

Bolt was only interested in playing the game. He wasn't listening to the one person who could help him with his game. And so it is in life. We often go our own way, ignoring the one person who can bless us in life and beyond. That person is Jesus who said, *"I am the Way, the Truth, and the Life. No one comes to the Father except through me."*[66] There is only one way to heaven and it's through Jesus. Many people ignorantly deny him. Many live in ignorance of the God who loves them and wants to save them.

The second story involves the greatest golf teacher ever, Harvey Penick. Early in his career Penick bought a red spiral notebook in which he jotted down observations about golf. He never showed the notebook to anyone except his son until 1991 when he shared it with a local writer and asked if he thought it was worth publishing. The man read it and told him that it would be a good book. He left word with Penick's wife the next evening that Simon & Schuster had agreed to an advance of $90,000.

The next time Penick saw the writer he seemed troubled. Finally and with great humility he said, *"With all our medical bills there's no way I can advance Simon & Schuster that much money."* The writer had to explain to Penick that he would be the one to receive the $90,000. That is much like the response many people have to the Gospel. It's

---

66 John 14:6

114

difficult to believe that such a fabulous gift could be free. Instead they ask, *"What will it cost me?"*

Sandra would have you know, you don't have to do anything. You only have to believe Jesus. Of course she would encourage you to love Jesus and follow Him as she did. This is the Gospel that Sandra believed and loved and lived. This is the truth she rested her life on. I know she would say to you today, *"Don't leave this place until you know that you are sure of your eternal life"*.

Example Seven: For an infant death.

There are parts of my job at which I feel skilled and competent. Right now is not one of them. I can't quite imagine the pain you must feel. The loss of a child must be one of the greatest of tragedies. You have lost part of yourself. I know that nothing I say this morning will take away your pain. I certainly can't bring him back. I can't tell you what his life might have been, or what he would have done. I can only encourage you to look to God. Right now that seems wrong. Why did God allow this boy to die? Does He really care? Is He really there?

One of the Bible writers wrestled with these thoughts: *"To You, O Lord, I lift my soul. In You I trust, O My God. Turn to me and be gracious to me for I am lonely and afflicted. The troubles of my heart have multiplied. Free me from my anguish. Look upon my affliction and my distress and take away all my sin."*[67]

David experienced a life of extreme highs and lows. Sometimes everything was right in his world, and at other times it could get no worse. So he expressed his emotions in the Psalms, and he let God raise him up when life was low.

I've learned some things about God. I've learned that God loves us, each of us, including Kevin. It is never God's will that anyone would die. God desires life. Death is the result of sin in our world. Not any particular sin, as if someone is directly responsible for Kevin's death. But sin in general brings death.

Still God loves us and desires to protect us from that consequence of sin. He accepted the responsibility for our sin when He became a man and died on the cross. He allowed Himself to die physically so that we would not die spiritually. Death for us is only a transition into eternal life. The body of Kevin may have died, but he lives on. God is in touch with our feelings. He experienced the loss of His son. He experienced death. Truly He knows what you feel today, and He does so because He loves you.

---

67   Psalm 25:16–18

I've learned that children have a special place in the Kingdom of God. People often wonder what happens to children who die. There is a wonderful episode in Jesus' life that tells us how important they are to Him. *"People were bringing little children to Jesus to have Him touch them, but the disciples rebuked them. When Jesus saw this He was indignant. He said to them. 'Let the little children come to me, and do not hinder them, for the Kingdom of God belongs to such as these.' And He took the children in His arms, put His hands on them, and blessed them."*[68]

God loves children, perhaps more than all others. They are innocent and trusting, honest and loving. God holds no sin against children who are not of an age to commit sin. The Bible clearly teaches that God holds each person responsible for his own sin. Rather than turn children away God welcomes them into His kingdom.

No one is more secure in God's arms than a child. At this very moment, Kevin rests in the comfort and safety of the loving arms of our Savior. There is no better place.

---

68   Mark 10:14–16

Example Eight: For the death of a cognitively impaired individual.

In our church we have several men who have cognitive impairments. They bring a special element to Agape Christian Church. Their love for Jesus and His church have taught me some things that I knew as Bible principles, but now I understand in a more practical way because of these men. Let me share three lessons with you:

First, we should all speak only positive and uplifting things to our friends and fellow church members. The Bible says, *"Do not let any unwholesome talk come out of your mouths, but only what is helpful for building others up according to their needs, that it may benefit those who listen."*[69] These beautiful children of God don't say hurtful or negative things to us at church or when we see them about town. I know Ricky could get acidic with family and some of you who work closely with him, but he quickly felt bad and apologized. When he encountered me or other church members, he always said positive and uplifting things. He encouraged me and tried always to build me up. He always asked me about the teams we both cheer for.

Someone might ask, *"Is that all he talks about, sports?"* No it's not, but Ricky knew that sports are fun and make people feel good. And his passion showed when he talked about the Bears or Cubs or the La Porte Slicers.

Sometimes I hear unwholesome talk from other church members, negative and even hurtful things said about or to someone. Sometimes I get drawn into it myself. In the ten or so years that I've known Ricky and these other brothers in Christ, not once have I heard ungodly things come out of their mouths. Wouldn't it be great if we all learned to speak only what is helpful for building others up according to their needs and what would benefit those who listen?

Second, we can learn from these men that we should never worry about what other people think of us when we worship. I'm usually up front when our church worships. I play guitar and lead the congregational singing. I can see everybody. I see how they

---

69 Ephesians 4:29

express themselves, or how they don't. Andy and David, Peter and William, and Ricky aren't worried about how they might look to someone else. They raise their hands, they clap, they move with the music even if not in rhythm. Whatever they feel they simply express. Sometimes they clap but they're a little bit off the beat and it makes me laugh but it's not a laughter of derision. It's pure joy because I see them worshiping honestly and without ego.

It has always been one of my weaknesses that I get self–conscious when I'm expressive. *"What if I look funny? People might think I'm silly."* I'm not alone. Being self–conscious holds a lot of people back from openly expressing the joy of worship. We would do well to learn from these men. The Bible encourages believers to raise our hands, to clap, to dance in worship. So what if the people around us think it's not dignified enough? I've learned that I'd rather be open and expressive like these men than uptight like so many others.

Third, we should all learn to accept Jesus with the pure innocence of a child. One time Jesus was teaching and people were bringing their children to meet Him. *"People were bringing little children to Jesus to have Him touch them, but the disciples rebuked them. When Jesus saw this, He was indignant. He said to them, 'Let the little children come to me, and do not hinder them, for the kingdom of God belongs to such as these. I tell you the truth, anyone who will not receive the kingdom of God like a little child will never enter it.' And He took the children in His arms, put His hands on them and blessed them."*[70]

I used to have a superficial understanding of this story. I thought that Jesus was telling us to be sure to teach children about Him: bring them to Sunday school and Vacation Bible School and other things where they learn about Jesus. But as I got to know these men, I started to see the importance of this sentence, *"I tell you the truth, anyone who will not receive the kingdom of God like a little child will never enter it."*[71]

---

70 Mark 10:13–16
71 Mark 10:15

A couple of things come to mind. First is the pure innocence of how they accept Jesus. There's no ego involved. It's not about them, it's about Jesus. They don't accept Christ with preconceived ideas about what should be. They don't bring their own requirements to the Kingdom of God. Like the little children in the Bible story, they just come to enjoy Jesus. They love His people and enjoy the fellowship of the church.

The second thing that comes to my mind is that they don't make a big deal out of deep theological issues. You might say, *"Well they don't understand theology"*. And maybe you're right, but who among of us does understand theology? I consider myself to be a pretty good Bible student and I have a good grasp of theology, but I've not found that my education results in the kind of unity with other Christians that these guys know.

Don't get me wrong. I think it's good for Christians to be educated in the Bible and to consider the truths of theology. But what draws us close to God and to each other is our common love of Jesus. It's not how smart we are or how well we can articulate what we believe. It's the simple fact that we love Jesus and we know that Jesus loves us.

Because Ricky accepted Jesus like a little child, we can be sure that he was welcomed into the Kingdom of God. Know this; he doesn't have any impairments anymore; he doesn't have the obstacles that made life more difficult for him than for many of us; he doesn't have limitations.

Today Ricky is at home with Jesus. Let us not mourn for him. Grieve if you must, that you have lost a friend, a brother, a son. But grieve not for Ricky because he's not dead, he is alive in Jesus Christ. This game is now over, but the season goes on. Go now and live for Jesus.

Example Nine: For a suicide.

Prayer

There are some circumstances in life for which you can't prepare. You can't really practice. And you can't know. When they arrive you just have to work your way through them. This is one of those circumstances. Mike put it well the other day, *"It sucks."* It sucks because there's nothing we can do to change it. It sucks because there's nothing we could have done to prevent it. It sucks because we know it didn't have to be. And most of all it sucks because our hearts are broken for Ben that he experienced such pain.

We're here today because a son, a brother, a friend, a grandson, a nephew, a good guy lost an insidious battle with depression and loneliness. The Bible says, *"Our enemy, the Devil, prowls around like a roaring lion looking for someone to devour."*[72] Satan has one goal, to deny God His due glory by destroying His relationship with His children. Sometimes Satan wins the battle on Earth,

Ben is not the first nor will he be the last man of God to succumb to Satan's lies. He is not the first nor will he be the last to experience depression so low that even his faith in our loving God couldn't pull him out.

Moses listened to constant complaining from the Israelites as he led them through the desert until he was ready to quit.

Elijah actually said to God *"...I have had enough, Lord, take my life"*[73]

Job lamented even being born, *"May the day of my birth perish. May that day turn to darkness. May that night be barren."*[74]

---

72 First Peter 5:8

73 First Kings 19:4b

74 Job 3:3–4

Even David, the man after God's own heart, felt the weight of despair, *"How long, O Lord? Will you forget me forever? How long will you hide your face from me? How long must I wrestle with my thoughts and every day have sorrow in my heart?"*[75] *"Be merciful to me, O Lord, for I am in distress. My eyes grow weak with sorrow . . . My life is consumed by anguish and my years by groaning . . . I am a dread to my friends."*[76] The Apostle Paul wrote, *"(I was) under great pressure, far beyond (my) ability to endure, so that (I) despaired even of life."*[77] Sometimes Satan wins the battle on Earth, but he does not win in eternity.

Today we remember a young man who grew up in this very church. A young man who worked hard to develop his skills and knowledge to make himself a valued employee with significant responsibilities with Cummings Engines. A friend with whom many fun times were shared. A son well loved by his family but too private to share his innermost struggles. A brother, the opponent in a few familial battles but whom you would fight for against any enemy.

Ben made a careful, and to him rational decision that ended his life but left us with the pain of a terrible loss, and questions without answers. He was *"tired of being tired"* and saw no relief.

So many here today love Ben and had you known would have been there for him. Sometimes you just can't help. You couldn't know what was going on inside of Ben unless he told you, and he didn't. You, his family, loved him and made sure he knew your love. But he lived a long way from here so you didn't know his struggles. You did your best. That's all you can do.

---

75   Psalm 13:1–2
76   Psalm 31:9–11
77   Second Corinthians 1:8

Appendix C
Examples of Committal Services

Example One:

Eternal Life

On a clear night if you look up carefully, you can see a satellite moving swiftly through the canopy of stars. There are many that are visible. One such, was placed in orbit 1900 miles above the Earth, by an outfit called the Celestis Group. They got permission from the U.S. Government to launch a satellite in 1985. First they got 10,330 families to pay a rather handsome price to have the ashes of their loved ones placed in the nosecone of the satellite. They promised eternal rest for all these people.

The truth is that the Celestis Group couldn't promise eternal rest, for in only sixty–three million years the orbit of that satellite will deteriorate and it will drop from space. But long after that satellite has burned up on re–entry into Earth's atmosphere, Jane Doe, and all who are in Christ will still be living in the glory of the presence of God.

Example Two: To remind guests that our Earthly bodies are not all there is[78]

In 2008 Readers Digest printed a story from a woman who told of driving with her two young boys to a funeral. She wrote that she had tried to prepare them by talking about burial and what we believe happens after death. The boys behaved well during the service, but at the gravesite she discovered her explanations weren't as thorough as she'd thought. The woman went on to tell how her four year old, in a loud and curious voice asked *"What's in the box?"*

---

78   I found this in a Reader's Digest, 2008

The answer to that question tells a lot about what we believe. I don't believe Dick is in that box. His body is in there but Dick is finished with this body. Now he has moved on to eternal life. God promises that life on earth is not the end if we believe in Him. There is prepared for us a home in Heaven in the presence of God. I pray that you will find comfort in this promise.

Example Three:

The Body, a Shell

Look around. All these stones, each one marking the final resting place of someone's body. In the coming weeks and years people will come here with flowers to honor and remember the people buried here. It's probably good. It helps them deal with their loss. You may choose to do so yourself. But remember, this is only the location of a body. The person is somewhere else. Dick's body will be here, but he won't. He lived in this shell for sixty–three years. Now he lives with Jesus in a new body. The Bible tells us clearly, Jesus will return to Earth one day. When He does He'll first gather up all believers who have died, then He'll bring us into the reunion, and we will be with Him for eternity.

Example Four: A Poem for a Christian[79]

Don't grieve. Be happy for those who have gone before us. Celebrate their passing with the faith they taught you, the love they've shown you, and the hope they had for your own happiness. It's okay to cry. Rain heals the Earth and tears heal the soul. Live a long life and give unending life to her by sharing her faith with the lost, giving her love to the lonely, and sow hope in those who have none.

---

79   Written by a friend, Phillip Briskey.

Example Five:

Psalm 103:15

"As for man, his days are like grass. He flourishes like a flower in the field. The wind blows over it and it is gone. And its place remembers it no more. But from everlasting to everlasting, The Lord's love is with those who fear Him."[80]

Life on Earth, even 100 years, is short. After we're gone, though people will remember us, the world goes on as if we had never been. But God never quits loving us. He loves us individually and eternally.

We now commit the body of Fiona May Brewer to the earth. The spirit we leave with God, for we know that the judge of all the Earth will do what is right.

---

80   Psalm 103:15

Appendix D
Premarital Counseling

There is no perfect one–size–fits–all plan for helping a couple prepare for marriage. Younger people are in for more surprises than are older couples, but even they, unless they have been previously married will experience new things they probably have not anticipated. Your goal is to give them insight into the changes that come when two individuals begin to live in real intimacy. Even if both of their parents enjoyed great marriages they are still probably not fully prepared for blending their attitudes and habits. If you are going to do premarital counseling you need to establish some plans for your role.

Before you begin premarital counseling you will have to consider what you believe the couple needs to hear. They may tell you of trouble areas but most likely you will have to determine what is important based on your initial interview with and knowledge of the couple. Are they going to talk or are they primarily listeners? Some couples (more often men than women) will not truly open up. Some of what follows will help encourage the couple to express their thoughts and attitudes and discuss differences. How many sessions will you do with the couple? "Contract" with them for a determined number of sessions.

To facilitate discussion I have included worksheets as useful tools to get a couple talking about specific issues.[81] I send one with the couple at the conclusion of our initial interview and then another when we set the next session. I ask them to do the worksheets sepa-

---

81   This idea is not original with me. A friend shared the idea (I do not know if he created it) while I was actively developing a plan for premarital counseling. I cannot locate an original creator(s). I have written my own questions but I doubt that they are much different from what anyone else would write. I chose also to use the idea of preparing written covenants to aid the couple in remembering the commitments we discuss.

rately. Then we will look through them together. Some couples will "cheat" by comparing their answers but it does not really matter. The point is to get them to talk about the issues. You will be able to quickly tell if they are not being completely honest in their responses. Also included are covenants that I ask the couple to agree to after discussing the issues. To discuss every answer to every question will make for very long sessions or very many sessions. Be careful choosing which questions you will discuss.

Part one, including worksheets 1–3 concerns personal and family attitudes. Part two, including worksheets 4–7 concerns attitudes about money. In case you do not already know, money issues are probably one of the most common area of discord in marriage. Part three, including worksheets 8 and 9 concerns relationships. Part four, worksheet number 10 concerns communication and conflict resolution, another common problem area for marriage. Part five, including worksheets 11 and 12, concerns sexuality in marriage. I have also inserted some of the teaching I have developed specifically for certain issues. I have found this teaching to be helpful. There are several covenants I ask the couple to commit to as part of their marriage covenant.

Part One: Family Attitudes

Worksheet One: Attitudes you may be bringing into your marriage.

Are the following statements true of your family?

1. We did not allow beer or alcohol in the house.
2. Hugging and touching were common at our house.
3. We liked to celebrate holidays as a family.
4. My parents put the needs of children before their own.
5. We valued promptness.
6. My Mom and Dad enjoyed a separate night out now and then.
7. We kept the house neat, orderly, and clean.
8. My parents attended our activities as often as possible.
9. We often believed we were being treated unfairly.
10. We believed in hard work and loyalty.
11. Family meals were important.
12. My father was head of the household.
13. We loved having friends and family visit.
14. We believed getting drunk is wrong.
15. Household chores were divided equally among us.
16. We were church attenders.
17. Both parents worked to provide income.
18. Dad taught us how to maintain cars and the yard.
19. My Dad doted on Mom.
20. Divorce was not in our vocabulary.

Worksheet Two: Attitudes you are bringing into your marriage.

Do these statements reflect your personal attitude?

1. I want our friends and family to visit often.
2. I want us to share equally in providing income.
3. I want us to be present at our children's activities.
4. I don't want to live close to my parents.
5. I will change jobs often for more pay.
6. I will pursue nights out with my friends, including friends of the opposite sex.
7. I will help with grocery shopping.
8. I don't like to be late or to leave at the last minute.
9. I will share in taking care of the home.
10. Regular private time is good for us.
11. Some alcohol is alright with me.
12. I believe marriage is forever.
13. I believe we should each have a hobby.
14. I want you to have your own career.
15. I dislike drunkenness or drug use.
16. Life is unfair.
17. We should remain close to our parents.
18. Separate vacations are OK with me.
19. Spontaneity is preferable to a definite schedule.
20. I'd rather not eat leftovers.
21. We should always celebrate birthdays and holidays.
22. I believe going to church together is important.
23. Back talk from children is not acceptable.
24. I do not want separate checking accounts.
25. We should work to be financially successful.

Worksheet Three: Determine who should do what in our marriage.

Who will . . .

1. Shop for groceries?
2. Attend to sick children?
3. Buy insurance?
4. Go to school activities?
5. Take care of the lawn?
6. Help with homework?
7. Handle bill paying?
8. Be responsible for discipline?
9. Buy the cars?
10. Decide which church to attend?
11. Take out trash?
12. Make beds?
13. Take the children to the dentist or doctor?
14. Find a house to live in?
15. Arrange and coordinate social activities?

Part Two: Financial Attitudes

Worksheet Four: Family attitudes about finances you may be bringing into your marriage.

Are the following statements true of your family?

1. We had clear financial goals.

2. We resisted debt.

3. My parents fought about money.

4. We kept a substantial savings account for emergencies.

5. We believed in tithing.

6. We did not borrow money for vacations.

7. My father provided for our family.

8. We struggled financially.

9. We were taught to give good tips for a wait staff.

10. We had a family budget.

11. We trusted God's principles for money decisions.

12. My parents seldom used credit cards.

13. My Dad put his job before the family.

14. My mother paid the bills.

15. We were taught to pay all bills when due.

Worksheet Five: Attitudes about finances you are bringing into your marriage.

Do these statements reflect your personal attitude?

1. I believe bankruptcy is acceptable.
2. I believe we should have and follow a budget.
3. We should have clear financial goals.
4. We should never carry a credit card balance.
5. We should only have joint accounts.
6. We should have a will.
7. We should use credit cards sparingly.
8. We should be open with our children about our finances.
9. We should save for emergencies.
10. We should each always have some cash on hand.
11. I believe it is OK to borrow money from friends.
12. We should not have to ask each other for money.
13. We should not lend money to a friend or relative without asking each other.
14. We should put our time together before our jobs.
15. We will tithe our income.
16. We can both be involved in paying bills.
17. We should decide together about moving for a job transfer.
18. We should pursue being debt free.
19. We should pay bills when due.
20. We should be conscious of God's instructions about money.

Worksheet Six: Determine the following before marriage.

1. Will you both work after your marriage?
2. Will one of you stay home after children are born?
3. Who will manage money at home?
4. Will you try to save money?
5. Will you plan to buy a house?
6. Will you have life insurance?
7. Will you have medical insurance?
8. Will you have household insurance?
9. Will you have and use credit cards?
10. Will you have separate checking/savings accounts?

Worksheet Seven: Discuss the following issues relating to money matters.

How important are the following?

1. Automobiles
2. Buying a house
3. Giving to charities
4. Giving to church
5. Education
6. Food
7. Furniture
8. Gifts for family
9. Gifts for friends
10. Having children
11. Health care
12. Hobbies
13. Insurance
14. Investments
15. Recreation
16. Avoiding debt
17. Retirement
18. Savings
19. Travel
20. Stylish clothing

Will you each agree to this Financial Covenant as part of your marriage?

1. I will never let money come before our relationship.

2. I will always be open and honest about our money matters.

3. If I am becoming irresponsible about money matters I will let you hold me accountable.

4. I will stay within our mutually established budget.

5. All money will be our money.

6. We will agree together on how to pay bills.

7. My wants and needs will be our wants and needs.

8. We will consult together before making major purchases.

9. I will take responsibility for how I handle our money.

10. If for any reason our financial situation ever becomes a problem that we cannot handle, I will go with you and get professional help.

I agree to this Financial Covenant because I love you and respect you and want only the best for us in our marriage.

Part Three: Relationships

Worksheet Eight: Family attitudes about relationships you may be bringing into your marriage.

Are the following statements true of your family?

1. We said "I love you" often.
2. Individual feelings were important.
3. We yelled as one way of getting what we wanted.
4. We complimented one another openly.
5. We argued and fought often.
6. We were expected to use manners like saying "Please" and "Thank you."
7. My parents listened to my opinions and tried to understand me.
8. My mother was in charge of the family.
9. My father had to have the last word on everything.
10. My father would set aside what he was doing and listen when we needed to talk.
11. My family recognized personal rights and privacy.
12. "Honesty is the best policy" ruled in our home.
13. We enjoyed playing together.
14. My parents listened to each other's opinion.
15. We did not keep secrets from one another.

Worksheet Nine:

Do these statements reflect your personal attitude?

1. I want you to respect and accept my feelings.
2. I think we can disagree without a fight.
3. Sometimes I am unwilling to share my real feelings.
4. I want us to avoid arguing.
5. I will listen attentively.
6. I think it is OK to talk about our married life with other people.
7. I trust that if I have a problem you will be beside me to help me.
8. Yelling causes me to withdraw.
9. I always want you to know that I trust you.
10. I think my way of expressing anger is acceptable.
11. I believe putting each other down or making fun will harm our marriage.
12. I will say, "I love you" by word and deed.
13. Compromise is healthy in our relationship.
14. We should plan a time for serious talks.
15. We should respect each other's thoughts and feelings.
16. I always want to know how you feel and what you think.
17. Criticism should be given carefully.
18. You have to be right all the time.
19. We should be able to express our thoughts openly and honestly.

20. If you sense that something bothers me and you ask me, "What's wrong?" I will often say, "Nothing".

21. The husband is head of the house.

22. I do not change my mind easily.

23. Your way of expressing anger is acceptable to me.

24. Keeping secrets from each other will not harm our marriage.

25. Helping each other draws us closer together.

26. I want you to value my thoughts and try to understand me.

27. If I am angry I don't want you to touch me.

28. You routinely interrupt me and dominate our conversations.

29. I am a not easy to talk to.

30. I always fear that if you don't get your way you will be angry with me.

Part Four: Communication
Worksheet Ten: When we communicate

My strength is . . .

My weakness is . . .

Your strength is . . .

Your weakness is . . .

The greatest strength of our relationship is . . .

Our greatest problem area is . . .

Will you each agree to this Communication Covenant as part of your marriage?

1. I agree to be as clear and open as possible.
2. I will turn off the TV and other distractions to give you my full attention.
3. I will be open and honest with you and allow you to be open and honest with me.
4. I will never call names, hit, or say "I don't love you."
5. I will allow you to disagree with me without getting angry.
6. I will take responsibility for my words and actions.
7. I will not speak for you unless I first consult you.
8. I will always be truthful with you.
9. I will pursue activities that will enrich our marriage.
10. If for any reason our communication seriously breaks down, I will go with you and get professional help.

I agree to this Communication Covenant because I love you and respect you and want only the best for us in our marriage.

Conflict Resolution

(I taught this material with lots of illustrations and further explanation on each step, allowing room for questions and comments.)

What I am going to share is a summation of the materials I have studied and learned. There is nothing unique it this. Any competent counselor will teach the same basic principles. The "Rules for Fair Fighting" are from the Bible, loosely based on Ephesians 4:25–32. Couples who are not Christian will not respond as positively as believers however they are workable principles for any conflict resolution process.

A couple must be clear about expectations, responsibilities, and the ways of handling differences in order to minimize misunderstanding and doubts. All marriage relationships will experience problems and conflicts. This is because no two people think and feel exactly the same on everything that matters. Two individuals with differing viewpoints, frames of reference, and values usually results in some pressure and heat. It is like M&Ms that the ads say "melt in your mouth but not in your hands." If you hold them tightly in your hands they *will* melt under the heat and pressure. Conflict free marriage is a myth, even for healthy, spiritual marriages. There is an old saying, "The problem is not the problem. The problem is how you handle the problem." How they handle conflicts and disagreements often will determine a couple's satisfaction with a marriage.

Couples who are unable to resolve a conflict or problem in their marriage get into trouble. Communication breaks down, and they get stuck on the problem. As a result intimacy suffers. They begin to pull away from each other, become defensive, and cease to trust each other fully. The foundations of the relationship are, at this point, crumbling. As you learn to resolve conflicts in your marriage in a healthy way, you will experience the joy and happiness God intends for you.

Differences between a man and wife are normal and not necessarily unhealthy. It is not a sign that happiness is lost. It merely means that you think differently. It is a sign that you are normal healthy individuals. If you never experience a conflict it may mean that you are repressing your feelings and are afraid to state your opinions. You may be refusing to be honest and vulnerable with each other.

Most people react to conflict in one of four ways. Some fight to win which causes the conflict to grow. Some surrender to find peace but the conflict is only buried for a time. Some withdraw. They pull back to regroup and rethink how they can better fight to win. The conflict is not resolved. In healthy relationships a couple seeks resolution. They find a way that they can both win. To disagree is normal. To resolve that disagreement because you love each other leads to lasting happiness and unity. This is the process you must learn.

Often the result of unresolved conflicts and problems is anger. Anger is a normal, natural emotion. Your ability to express it is fundamental to survival in relationship. When anger surfaces it is a signal that something is wrong. Anger is often experienced when needs or expectations are not met, goals are blocked or not reached, and values are trampled. A person feels hurt or taken advantage of. Many people respond to anger with venting. They will fight back, explode verbally or physically. This will heighten and intensify the anger and probably interfere with efforts to resolve the conflict.

Another common reaction is to suppress one's feelings. Seeking "peace at any price" one hopes that if left alone the problem will go away. This usually ends with someone withdrawing from the relationship. Eventually the problem will return, probably with an explosion of rage. In healthy relationships the conflict is met with careful processing, understanding each other, and finding a way to settle emotions so that through rational discussion a resolution can be reached.

While I dislike the term, I will teach you how to "fight fairly." To start I encourage you to commit that you will never hit, call names, or say "I don't love you," and never use the "D" word, divorce. These behaviors often coincide with anger and would be extremely damaging to your relationship. If nothing else they will leave your mate wondering if he or she can trust you anymore.

The ability to resolve conflict comfortably requires rational thinking mixed with creativity. You have to be able to step back from your problems, clearly define them, and search for options that you both are comfortable with.

Most fights are not fair. Instead of disagreeing agreeably most conflicts begin as tiffs, become arguments, turn into quarrels, and ultimately result in knock down drag out battles. To change that pattern I will teach eight "Rules for Fair Fighting."

Rule number one: Commit to honesty. This is more difficult in a fight than you might think and is a basic and essential behavior. There is no room for lies in a relationship. Dishonesty breaks down trust. You probably committed to honesty in your wedding preparation if not in your vows. The point of the conflict will shift whenever there is lying. With lying comes doubt. How can your mate know that anything you say is true? I encourage you to establish right now, before you marry, that you will always be honest. If you cannot make this commitment you should not marry.

Rule number two: Commit to respect. When you marry two become one. Your body is her body and her body is your body. You would not treat yourself with disrespect, nor should you treat your mate with disrespect, ever. Even in a dispute, respect your mate. Even if he or she does not respect you, you keep your end of this agreement.

Rule number three: Commit to avoid sin. Even when angry in a conflict there is no excuse for hurting your mate with unrelated issues. It is not unusual for someone to go off track with ugly accusations or characterizations, attacking the person instead of the

144

problem. Some will reject the other with comments like *"I hate when you do that,"* or create guilt by association saying *"you sound like your druggie brother."*

Similar attacks that may not be sin but are still damaging to the resolution process are bringing up past issues, *"remember when..."* If you have handled something before do not bring it up now. Another attack is becoming dramatic, especially getting emotional. Crying may be a way to manipulate the emotions of your mate. Making threats (suicide or divorce) is also unfair. Gross exaggerations are unfair. Try not to say *"you always"* or *"you never."* These attacks move the talk off the issue and away from the problem you are trying to resolve.

Rule number four: Commit to a time to fight. This is not about putting off resolution. It is about finding a good time to handle it. When you come through the door from fishing and your wife is making supper and the kids are fighting is probably not the time to say *"We need to talk."* Neither is it a good time when you come home from work tired and wanting some peace and quiet. When you are physically or emotionally drained or under outside stress is also not good for seeking resolution. I suggest that you make an appointment to "fight." I know it sounds silly but it does two things for you. First it allows you to step back and evaluate just how important the issue is, and second it gives you time to think carefully about how you can work together so that you both win. When the time is right do not let it pass.

Rule number five: Commit to offer positive solutions. Be prepared with ideas to resolve the issue. It is not good enough to point out another's faults or failures. If you want to resolve conflict, be prepared to share things you can both do to fix it.

Rule number six: Commit to speaking positively. Sometimes in the midst of a conflict one or the other will become loud or abusive. Some will use harsh words or get defensive. These will escalate the emotions and disrupt the spirit of resolution. Saying things that build up or encourage will help your mate relax knowing that your love still rules your relationship.

Rule number seven: Commit to fight in private. Never fight in public. Fighting in front of others embarrasses yourselves and others around you. Public fighting often reveals intimate secrets and personal flaws. This only increases the harm of the conflict.

Rule number eight: Commit to cleaning up the mess. When your conflict is over recognize that feelings have probably been hurt, egos damaged, and emotions frayed. This is a time to be kind and compassionate. Express forgiveness and reaffirm your love.

Keep in mind that there is an easy way to end an unfair fight. Quit! It's no fun to fight alone. If either of you is violating one of these eight rules, stop fighting and reestablish your commitment to resolving the real issue. If you are beaten (she was right), stop. Don't fight to the death.

Of course none of this will work unless you are both committed to resolving conflicts in a way that you both win.

Techniques for Conflict Resolution

(This is another way I teach about conflict resolution. The points are stated simply and I added many other thoughts as I taught.)

1. Understand that it is normal for two individuals to experience conflict.

2. Realize that anger is a cue that there is a problem indicating a need for resolution.

3. Plan a time to resolve a conflict. If emotions are out of control, step aside, regroup, calm down, think, and only then return to the discussion.

4. Define the problem to the best of your ability. Often a couple needs a counselor to see through the peripherals to the real issue.

5. Identify what each other is saying and thinking about the problem.

6. Discover areas of agreement and disagreement.

7. Stay on the subject.

8. Explore options for resolution.

9. Aim for a solution. Do not get stuck on the problem.

10. Value and respect your spouse by valuing and respecting her/his ideas and feelings.

11. Seek common goals. Find a way that you both win. Common goals in which you both win gives you direction for working together.

12. Identify each other's needs. Taking note of needs that are not being met will help you see the real issue. In your solution meet each other's needs.

13. Finish. When the conflict is settled in a satisfactory way finish with physical touch (hugs and kisses). This is an active indicator that you are OK to move on.

14. It's over. Do not bring it up again. It is solved. Leave it solved.

Will you each agree to this Conflict Resolution Covenant as part of your marriage?

1. I will respect your opinions and feelings.
2. I will be open and honest with you about my thoughts and feelings.
3. I will work with you to come to a resolution as soon as possible.
4. I will never hit.
5. I will never call names.
6. I will never say, "I don't love you".
7. I will never hate you.
8. I will take responsibility for my words and actions.
9. I will "fight fairly" and never unfairly.
10. If for any reason we come to a problem or disagreement we cannot resolve, I will go with you and get professional help.

I agree with this Conflict Resolution Covenant because I love you and want only the best for us in our marriage.

Part Five: Sexuality

(I taught this material with lots of illustrations and further explanation on each step, allowing room for questions and comments.)

While we want to pretend it is not true, in reality most of us know very little about sexuality before we get married. People who have been sexually active before marriage have an entirely different set of problems than a couple whose sex life begins on their wedding night. You will serve them by teaching about sexual intimacy. The next two worksheets can help lead you into this discussion. Before using these worksheets I offer the following teaching about sexuality in marriage. Please allow me this caveat: If a couple are not Christian they may not accept Biblical teaching about sex.

Men and Women Are Different

Men and women are different. Men do not decorate their written notes. Men scribble. Women use scented and colored stationary while dotting their "I's" with hearts. Before going shopping for groceries a woman makes a list. A man waits until he runs out of something then drives to the grocery store and buys whatever looks good at the time.

When a relationship breaks up a woman cries and pours her heart out to her friends. She writes a poem about how all men are idiots and how she hates men. Then she goes on with life, usually finding another. A man will not let go. He will pursue her begging for another chance before calling her ugly names and telling her how he never really liked her in the first place.

Women tend to mature faster than men. A seventeen year old woman can function as an adult. A seventeen year old man is still playing video games and giving atomic wedgies.

When a couple marries the man will bring four items to their bathroom, a toothbrush, a shaving kit, one bar of soap, and one towel. His new wife will bring a suitcase with about one hundred items, most of which her new husband has no idea what they are for.

A married woman with children will know everything about her children. She knows their school schedule, their dentist appointments, romances and best friends. Her husband is mildly aware that there are short people living in the house.

Of course these are generalizations but they make the point that men and women are very different. The differences between men and women often lead to conflicts in the marriage. Couples will fight over things that are nothing more than normal differences between the sexes. One of the big differences that often ends with conflict is sex. Men and women tend to be very different. Although it may be uncomfortable, allow me to talk about sex.

Sex should be fun. When God created the man and woman she was exactly like the man except for certain physical parts. The parts that are different are the source of some very good feelings. That is God's plan.

The prohibitions found in the Bible against certain types of sex are against sex outside of marriage. The Bible repeatedly speaks against sexual relations outside of marriage. Anything else is sin and destroys marriage.

The Bible tells of a time when King Abimelech, who apparently had been interested in Isaac's wife Rebekah, saw the couple engaged in sex. The text says he saw Isaac "sporting" with his wife (Gen. 26:8). The word "sporting," sometimes translated "caressing," comes from the same root as Isaac's name meaning laughter. It seems they were having a very good time.

Sex is supposed to be fun, but it is not fun when a couple does not agree on what sex should be. I think the reason this gets messed up is that we are so different and men and women just do not often take the time to really understand each other. They just assume they

150

know, but they are usually wrong because they have never really considered it and they are embarrassed to study it.

Sex is for marriage. The Apostle Paul offered some extraordinary teaching about this. *"Since there is so much immorality, each man should have his own wife and each woman her own husband."*[82] Paul understood the power of the sex drive, and he knew that there was much immorality, people having sex without a marriage commitment, he taught that a couple should have sex only with their spouse.

A husband or wife who deprives his or her spouse of this pleasure is preparing the conditions for Satan to exploit and tempt the partner to sin. There is no condemnation against sex in marriage. The solution for the power of the sex drive is for a couple to marry and enjoy sex within that bond.

Sex in marriage is a right and an obligation. This is where it gets tricky. *"The husband should fulfill his marital duty to his wife, and likewise the wife to her husband."*[83] A key word is *"fulfill"* or *"give to"*. It is an imperative, perhaps a command. Another key word is "marital duty." It means something that is owed. Husbands and wives owe it to each other to enjoy sex. Married women and men have a right to expect that they will have sex with their spouse. There is no religious benefit and nothing to be gained from celibacy in marriage.

You do not have a right to make unilateral decisions about sex in marriage, either demanding or withholding it. This does not mean you have to have sex whenever the other wants it whether you want to or not. If one of you does not want to have sex there is a problem with your love and if that is the case you should seek help. Married people ought to enjoy sex but it is not something that should be enjoyed at the other's expense. It should be mutually enjoyed. If that is not happening you should get help to fix the problem.

You belong to each other. Paul continued writing, *"The wife's body does not belong to her alone but also to her husband. In the same way,*

---

82   First Corinthians 7:2
83   First Corinthians 7:3

the husband's body does not belong to him alone but also to his wife."[84] This is not a commandment. It is a statement. It was common in that world to assume that the husband owned the rights to his wife's body but Paul's teaching goes beyond the norm to say that the wife owns the rights to her husband's body. Paul articulated a very different view of marriage sex than what was normally taught. Marriage is a relationship of mutual submission (Ephesians 5:21).

Sex is a very important part of marriage and couples should only refrain from having sex by mutual consent. Listen to Paul's words in verse five, *"Do not deprive each other except by mutual consent and for a time, so that you may devote yourselves to prayer. Then come together again so that Satan will not tempt you because of your lack of self–control."*[85] To withhold sexual relations may be robbing or stealing a part of marriage from your spouse. Sex is important because, unless it is abused or misused, it draws a couple together.

The Apostle understood that sometimes, when the relationship is strained, sex is not enjoyable. The cure is not to forced sex because *"the Bible says we are supposed to have sex."* Listen carefully to me. Most husbands are happy to have sex with their wives even if they are angry or troubled in some way. Most wives have no interest in sex unless the relationship is right. The cure is to find the problem and fix it. When the relationship is broken in some way, sex loses its glamor. When the relationship is made right, sex can be enjoyed again.

Four conditions are given that should govern any moratorium or suspension of sex in marriage: *By mutual consent.* The word is symphonic, like an orchestra all playing the same piece. Another condition is that *it is for a time.* There is a special circumstance that leads to a couple refraining from sex, obviously to fix a broken relationship as understood from the third condition *that they may have leisure to pray.* It is not just because one does not want to have sex, it is in order that they can pray about whatever issue is blocking their

---

84   First Corinthians 7:4
85   First Corinthians 7:5

normal sex lives. Finally *they are intended to come together again*, that is return to normal sexual relations. Failing to recognize a problem but simply withholding sex will give Satan an opportunity to tempt the couple into immorality.

Working with couples as I have and by careful study as a pastoral counselor I have learned what sex generally means to husbands and what it means to wives:

Sex satisfies a man's sex drive. Regardless of how Hollywood portrays it, males usually have a stronger sex drive than females. This tends to be true throughout the animal world. For humans it is a gift from God to motivate oneness and reproduction. Wild male animals do not think about having children. They just want to have sex. That often leads to their demise. Men are a lot like that. They are not usually thinking about having children. They just want to have sex.

Sex fulfills a man's manhood. Men have strong egos. If a man is not a man in his own eyes he will find ways to make himself a man. His sex drive is linked to that ego. A man can fail at academics, at his profession, even in social life, and still be strong as long as his wife wants him. But if he fails there, other successes ring hollow.

Sex enhances his love for his wife. A man can find sex just about anywhere and anytime. Many men do. Only legitimate sex with his wife will satisfy him without guilt. Men who are loved at home do not seek for it elsewhere. His love for his wife grows as their sex life grows.

Sex reduces friction at home. Little irritations that unsettle a home are less of a problem when a man's love life is good. It is like everything he puts up with at work or even at home is worth it if he knows his wife loves him and wants to have sex with him.

Again generally speaking, sex helps a wife fulfill womanhood. Women want to know they are attractive to men. Every wife wants to know that her husband is turned on by her and that he truly wants to please her. If sex is unfulfilling it complicates her self–image. If she feels that she is unsuccessful with her husband she will feel less of a woman.

Sex reassures a wife of her husband's love. People have a basic need to be loved, even those who pretend that they do not. This is generally true more of women than men. A wife wants to know that her husband loves her. She does not want him to use her for sex. She wants him to love her. Men must be careful here because we can be quite uncaring when we seek to satisfy our own desires without considering what matters to our wives.

Sex satisfies her sex drive. Women do have sex drive, usually different than that of men and often less demanding, but it is real. Again the entertainment industry wants us to believe women are insatiable. In my years of counseling I have yet to meet a women who could not get enough and did not care with whom as long as she had sex. None–the–less women, just like men, have a sex drive and it is best satisfied in married love.

Finally, sex helps her relax. Tim and Beverly LaHaye have taught that the female reproductive system is intrinsically connected to her nervous system. It is beyond my expertise but according to the LaHayes it was God's design that a woman who enjoys relaxing sexual experiences in marriage will find that these experiences help relax her nervous system.

There are two ways we can destroy the beauty of sex in marriage. One is to ignore God's precepts and do things our own way, make our own rules, make sex the pursuit of lust rather than an act of love. A second way is to act selfishly, using sex to please ourselves perhaps at the expense of our mates.

Worksheet Eleven: Family attitudes about sex you may be bringing into your marriage.

Are the following statements true of your family?

1. We did not talk about sex.
2. My Dad believed that sex was a cure for every problem with my mother.
3. My parents enjoyed a loving relationship.
4. My father used crude language about sexual things.
5. My parents hugged and kissed in front of us.
6. My father clearly thought my mother was attractive.
7. We were taught a different sexual standard for women than for men.
8. Sex was mother's wifely duty.
9. My parents believed they should be sexually faithful to their marriage.
10. My parents talked to me about sexual issues.
11. My father said loving things to my mother.
12. My parents fought about sex.
13. I never felt comfortable asking my parents about sex.
14. My parents always put each other first.
15. As I developed sexually my parents were positive and encouraging.

Worksheet Twelve: What I think about sex.

Do these statements reflect your attitude?

1. My spouse should always be willing to submit to my sexual needs.
2. I want my spouse to share if what I do causes discomfort.
3. I want to know how to please my spouse.
4. I want us to continue dating regularly after we are married.
5. I will keep physically clean for my mate.
6. It is absolutely necessary that we are both faithful in marriage.
7. Setting the mood should precede sex.
8. I was sexually abused as a child.
9. I have some fear of sex.
10. We should feel free to talk about our sex life with friends.
11. Public display of affection is OK with me.
12. I find it difficult to talk about sex.
13. The wife is responsible for birth control.
14. It is OK for the wife to initiate sexual activity.
15. I understand a woman's menstrual period and how that will affect sex.

Sexual Relationship Covenant

Will you each agree to this Sexual Relations Covenant as part of your marriage?

1. I will always be faithful to you and you alone.

2. I will be open and honest talking about our sexual relationship.

3. I want you to always tell me what pleases you.

4. I will tell you if something does not please me because I love you and want to have the best sexual relationship we can.

5. I agree to let you guide me and I am willing to follow.

6. I will not talk about our private sex life with anyone else.

7. I will not use sex as a weapon.

8. I will not criticize or make fun of your sexuality.

9. If for any reason we come to a sexual problem we cannot solve, I will go with you to get professional help.

10. I trust God's teaching and guidelines about sexual relationships and agree to make them a part of our marriage.

I agree with this Sexual Relationship Covenant because I love you and want only the best for us in our marriage.

Other specific teaching you may choose to offer in premarital counseling include:

- Intimacy and communication
- How to keep your marriage vibrant
- Understanding how love is expressed[86]

An extremely helpful tool I have used is *The Seven Habits of Highly Effective Families*[87]. Stemming from his original *The Seven Habits of Highly Effective People* and using the same seven concepts, this version focuses specifically on families. To learn the concepts and teach them to a couple you are counseling is a great way to set them up for a good marriage.

I also taught "The Personalities" from the book *Personality Plus*[88]. My wife, being a certified instructor in "The Personalities," helps me with this. If you do not have an expert handy you can read the book, learn the material yourself, and share it with your clients. (Knowing "The Personalities" will help *you* in all of your relationships.)

Having counselled many couples over 40 years of ministry I have put together some graphic and direct teaching about the differences between men and women. I met privately with the woman teaching about men, and then with the man teaching about women. I realize that we all like to think we know about the opposite sex, but I have found that most do not really know. It tended to be quite personal so I was careful with the many illustrations I used to add clarity to the teaching.

---

86   Swihart, *How Do You Say "I Love You?"*, and Chapman, *Five Love Languages*.
87   Covey, *Seven Habits of Highly Effective Families*.
88   Littauer, *Personality Plus*.

I gave a copy to each, encouraging to keep it safe and refer to it often. It can help avoid major pitfalls that have doomed many marriages.

For men:

(This material also was enhanced with illustrations and further explanation, again allowing room for questions and comments.)

Marriage Does not Come With a Manual, but This Comes Close

I did not get any kind of manual for being a husband when I got married. Apparently it was out of stock that year. All I got was what I learned watching my parents and a few other couples. I observed some behaviors that I liked and some I did not. I saw happiness and fighting. Between witnessing marriages, counseling marriages, and being married, I have learned much and wish to share some wisdom before you tie the knot. Choose for yourself what you will apply.

Encourage your wife. Make a point of knowing what her dreams are. Ask her. She wants you to support her and care about her life. She wants to know she matters to you. Encourage her to pursue her dreams. If you do not she will probably resent you.

Be the spiritual leader of your home. Your wife (and children) want you to lead your family. Note that there is a difference between being a leader and being in control. Do not lead from behind. Take a stand, especially on spiritual matters. This is what the Bible means when it says *"the husband is the head of the wife"*[89]. Do not leave spiritual leadership to your wife.

Do not look at pornography. While viewing pornography is not the same as adultery, it introduces many of the same problems and feelings. It will affect how you see your wife. It will cause her to doubt your affection for her. It often leads to pressuring her to do

---

89 Ephesians 5:23

things she may not want. Give all of your sexual intimacy to your wife.

Have good male friends. Have some men in your life who talk positively about their wives. Enjoy friendships with men who are concerned to be ever better husbands.

When you are with them do not speak negatively of her. Speak so well of her that others might be jealous of your relationship.

Always speak to your wife in kindness. Remember the old yarn, *"If you don't have something good to say, say nothing at all."* That applies doubly to speaking to your wife. Praise what she does well. Show your appreciation for all that she does.

Participate in household chores. Do not leave it all to your wife as women's work. As part of your relationship you can negotiate who is primarily responsible for various chores, then help her with "her work". It does not really matter who does it. It must be done so help get it done. Show her you care about the entire household.

Find activities to do together. Ask her to participate in things you like to do and ask to participate in things she likes. Learn to understand why each other desires certain chosen activities. You want to share your whole life with her and you want to share her whole life.

Take care of yourself emotionally. Make sure it is OK for each of you to have things to do alone. As much as you want to be together all the time, most couples do well with some separate time. Do things for yourself that give you stability.

Take care of yourself physically Do not "let yourself go". She married you as you are. Do your best to maintain your health.

Be there. When you are with your wife, be there, not just in the room. Do not allow the TV, or your phone, or the internet to draw your attention away. Make sure you have special family time when nothing is allowed to interfere.

Love her. The most important woman in your child's life is his mother. Make sure he knows you love her first and foremost. Do not be afraid to display affection.

Physical contact. Do not leave physical touch exclusively to the bedroom. Hold her hand. Hug her. Sit beside her when watching TV. Keep her physically close when appropriate. The busyness of life often interferes with touch. Who has time for that? Make time. Remember no other man should be providing physical comfort and assurance. You and you alone have the right to her physical affection. She has the right to your physical affection.

Respect. Your wife needs to know that you respect her. Care about here desires and wishes. Never let her feel as a second class person next to you. Never let her think that she is not up to your standards. Throughout your marriage continue to seek to know what makes her tick. Make sure she knows she is an equal partner in your marriage.

Interact with her. Think about how you interact with and respond to other people in your life, friends and strangers. Be sure you interact with and respond to your wife better than you do others. It is easy to treat your spouse with less respect because you know she loves you and will forgive you if you fail. All the more reason to treat her with more respect than you do the other people in your life.

Burdens. When you said *"I do"* you married all of each other. That means her burdens are your burdens. Take them on. Help her carry them. Go through all of life together, whatever that means. When life gets tough, be strong for her. Be sure she knows that you will fight any battle for her.

Love language. Every person has a love language, sometimes more than one. Learn how she expresses love and express yours in her language. What makes her feel special and valued are probably different than what works for you. I recommend the books *The Five*

Love Languages and *How Do You Say 'I Love You?'*[90]   She will notice when you express your love in the way she sees love.

Space. When you love a woman you want to be with her always, often even to the point of smothering. Yes, you have become one, but she is still an individual and needs the space to be herself. In this she will enjoy a high sense of esteem and will bring that positivity to your relationship.

Know her. Early in your relationship you wanted to know everything about her. Why should that ever end? No, you do not know everything even after many years. Demonstrate your love by asking to learn more and more. Do not allow your relationship to drift apart. Ask any marriage counselor and you will be told that one of the most common problems in marriage is that a couple comes to where they don't know each other anymore. Make a point of knowing what is going on in each other's life. You married her as she is, not as she might be. Recognize who she is. As you both change in life it is important that you appreciate who she is "now". Change together.

Pray. Pray for her always and often. Pray for her needs. Pray for her wishes. Pray for her health. Pray for her anxieties. Pray for her joys, and her sorrows. Pray for her husband, that he will be the husband God knows she needs.

Effort. All of this takes effort. Whatever it takes to be the husband God intended for her, be that man. Do not worry if you are not receiving as much as you are giving. You love her, so give everything to her. Rare is the wife who will not respond in kind to the genuine and strong love of her husband. If you feel you are being cheated and begin to withhold effort for yourself, she will feel it and start to hold back also. It will be an ever descending spiral until the marriage is over. When you give full effort, since she does not have to look out for herself, she will have effort to expend on you. That is an ever ascending spiral, and it is wonderful.

---

90   Noted above.

162

Do's and Don'ts for Husbands

Things wives do not want their husbands to do.

- Do not "babysit" the kids. It is not babysitting when she watches them nor is it is when you watch them.

- Do not suggest that your work is more important than housework. She works hard maintaining your home. Recognize and appreciate her work.

- Do not give her a household appliance as a gift, unless she has specifically asked for it.

- Do not buy her the kind of perfume a hooker or cougar might use. No matter how sexy she is, she is not trying to attract men. She already has the one she loves.

- Do not talk as if she is not a good enough driver for you.

- Do not disregard a meal she worked hard to cook. No, she is not a classically trained chef, but she does not get paid nor does she have the time that a chef has.

- Do not stop caring about what you look like. She married a man she is impressed with, not a slug. Keep up with fashion or trust her to guide you.

- Do not act like you are the smartest person in the room and she is lucky to have you to educate her.

- Do not ignore her new hairdo. Notice when she changes.

- Do not behave as if the little bit of housework you do is your greatest gift to her. Household chores are yours too.

- Do not work so much you do not have time for the family. Find a balance. She would rather have you than a big house and fancy car.

- Do not come home and sit in front of the TV while she continues taking care of the house and kids.

- Do not act like your work is harder and matters more than hers.

- Do not criticize her in front of the kids or your friends and other people.

- Do not be selfish, even if you both agree that you are head of the household.

- Do not say you will do something and then procrastinate.

- Do not use your size to intimidate her.

- Do not act like you don't need to present yourself attractive to her.

- Do not act like you are listening when you are watching TV or your phone.

- Do not leave the discipline of the kids to her.

- Do not leave it to her to help the kids with homework.

- Do not shut her out of what is going on in your life. Do not say "Nothing" when she asks what is wrong.

- Do not express irritation when you disagree or when she errs.

- Do not react to her without thinking.

- Do not ever use the word "divorce". Once you say it, it is always out there.

- Do not avoid difficult conversations with her.

- Do not make major purchases without her.

- Do not stare at, ogle, or let your eyes linger on other women.
- Do not assume you know what she is thinking.
- Do not immediately try to solve her problems. Often she just wants you to listen.
- Do not lacerate her with sarcasm. It may be funny but it hurts.
- Do not treat her like your child. She is your partner.
- Do not try to control her. Guide her and help her.
- Never talk about your sex life with anyone else.
- Do not tell her she is supposed to submit to you.
- Never get your sexual appetite fulfilled by any source but her.
- Stop grabbing her butt, especially in public.
- Never be alone with another woman.
- Do not discuss your "problems" with another woman. Discuss them with her.
- Never keep the reality of your finances from her.
- Do not keep score of how often you make love.
- Do not make fun of her, even when she is not present.
- Do not let your other interests rob her of your leisure time unless you both agree.
- Do not act like you have done something difficult by putting clothes in the laundry.

For Women:

(As with the teaching for men, illustrations and further explanation were used, allowing room for questions and comments.)

Marriage Doesn't Come With a Manual, but This Comes Close

Many books have been written about married life, a number of which I have read. Most of what I think I know and what I teach about being a wife I learned by watching my parents and a few other couples, and by being married to a woman. Some behaviors I liked and some I did not. I saw happiness and I saw fighting. Between witnessing marriages, counseling marriages, and being married, I have learned much. I also asked some of the women of our church for their thoughts. I will share some wisdom before you tie the knot. Choose for yourself what you will apply.

Encourage your husband. He wants to be your Prince Charming. He wants to provide for and take care of you. He has dreams for your marriage. Ask him about his goals and dreams. Allow him to share his hopes and fears. Encourage his efforts to guide your family's future.

Support his role as spiritual leader of your family. Not all husbands want to lead, but that is his responsibility. Be careful not to undermine his role. If he fails to lead do not fight with him about it. You do what you must while continuing to encourage him to take the lead.

Enjoy friendships with other women. Choose them carefully. Seek women who speak well of their husbands and are not publically critical of them. Negative talk by your friends can put negative thoughts in your mind. Speak well of your husband. It is inappropriate to disparage your husband to your friends.

Build him up verbally. There is enough rudeness in our society. He does not need more from you. Make your home a refuge from the world; a place where he hears positive and kind things.

166

Do not say, "You never help out around the house!" Ask him to help you, then thank him when he does. It is wise to mutually agree on who is responsible for certain chores but all chores belong to both of you. Recognize that he sees taking care of your vehicles, the lawn, and the house itself as important as household chores.

Do activities together. Even if you may not enjoy his activities you can still do some with him. Learn about his interests and show some interest yourself. Show him that you care about what matters to him. If you do not you will miss some parts of his life.

Men tend to be visual creatures. Take care of your body, if not for yourself, do so for him. When he looks at you he sees the most beautiful woman he knows. He wants to see you this way. Do your best to be physically appealing to him. He wants to be turned on by you. He wants you to be sexy for him. It is not wise for you to be that way for other men. Your sexiness is a private thing between you and your husband.

Take care of your emotional self. Find hobbies or activities that recharge your emotions after being "a wife and mother," two very taxing roles. Have someone (a woman, never a man unless a professional counselor) that you can safely and privately talk to about yourself. I would suggest that you find someone who has been happily married for many years. Her wisdom will probably be invaluable.

Understand that he wants to relax when he first arrives home from work. Give him some time before unloading your day or expecting him to get started on his "honey–do" list. Bring up problems or issues only after he has had some time to decompress from his job.

Love him. He is the most important man in your children's lives. They want to know that their mother loves their father. Make sure he knows you love him more than any other. Do not be afraid to display affection.

Allow him to touch you. Obviously you do not want him groping you, especially in front of the children, but his love is strengthened when he hugs and kisses you. Hold his hand. Sit together when watching TV. He desires the physical touch of a woman. He has a right to your physical affection. Do not let another woman fulfill that need. Men who are fulfilled at home seldom stray looking for that touch.

Respect him. Respect his work, whatever that is. Never let him think he does not live up to your high standards. Make sure he knows you think he is the best.

Know him. You married him as he is, not as he might be. As he grows in life he changes. Pay attention to know who he is becoming. Do not expect him to be the same man you married however many years ago. Know how he communicates his love. Most men who work two jobs do it not to get away from their wives and families but to provide. That is his love language. I recommend the books *The Five Love Languages* and *How Do You Say 'I Love You?'*[91] If his love language causes harm to you, you need to tell him in a way that does not criticize him. When you understand his love language, love him that way.

Pay attention to your interactions. Be conscious of how you speak to him. He will not appreciate criticism or nagging. Do not heap praise on someone else's husband. That may make him feel put down or unappreciated. Treat him with as much respect as you would any other person.

Share his burdens. When you married you became one. His concerns and troubles are your concerns and troubles. This is "going through life together." Build each other up and fight every battle together.

Do not fight with him, especially if he has troubles at work. Realize it is difficult to fight battles at work and also at home. Do not

---

91   Noted above.

let your home become another battleground. Do your best to make your home a refuge.

Never stop learning about him. Talk often. Ask him about his life. Often marriages that fall apart do so because a couple quit learning about each other. You need to know what is going on in each other's lives. Nothing should be off limits. You married all of him so you should want to know who he is.

Pray for him. Being the husband of a wonderful woman is not easy. Most husbands I know feel inadequate to live up to what you deserve. We tend to believe we "married up." Pray for his emotions. Pray for his self–esteem. Pray for his labor, his joys, and his sorrows. Pray that his wife will be what God knows he needs.

Effort. All that I am saying here takes effort. Whatever it takes to be the wife God intended for him, be that woman. Do not worry if you are not receiving as much as you are giving. You love him, so give him everything you've got. Rare is the husband who will not respond in kind to the genuine and affectionate love of his wife. If you feel you are being cheated and begin to withhold effort for yourself, he will feel it and start to hold back effort for himself. It will be an ever descending spiral until the marriage is over. When you give full effort, since he does not have to look out for himself, he will have effort to expend on you. That is an ever ascending spiral, and it is wonderful.

Do's and Don'ts for Wives

Things husbands do not want their wives to do.

- Do not expect him to "mother" the children the way you do. He loves your kids even while doing so in a "manly" way.

- Do not disrespect his work. Even if it does not have the prestige of other jobs, or even if he hates it. It is his job.

- Do not tell him how attractive or important someone else is. Do not talk about how smart your friend's husband is.

- Do not criticize his hobbies and recreation.

- Do not belittle his lack of knowledge about tools and construction and cars.

- Do not take for granted that he finds you attractive. He appreciates that you make yourself look great for him.

- Do not talk about how much you "love" a certain actor, athlete, or musician.

- Do not ignore that he finds you sexy. Be sexy for him.

- Do not get angry if he does not answer a question immediately. He wants to think about it before he speaks.

- Do not mother him as if he were one of the children.

What Men Want

- Do not put so much effort into the house that you have nothing left for him.

- Do not talk about how great your friend's husband is.

- Do not criticizing him, especially in front of the kids.

- Do not nag him to get the "honey–do" list finished.

- Do not treat him as if he will be unhappy with you if you do not do everything his way.

- If something is bothering you, tell him.

- Do not manipulate him by crying or pouting when you do not get your way.

- Do not let the kids control you because you do not want to discipline them when necessary.

- Do not keep the kids' behavior from him. He wants to know.

- Do not ignore your "looks." He likes that you are pretty.

- Do not get angry when you disagree, and do not act like you do not love him anymore.

- Do not schedule for him without first speaking with him.

- Understand that he wants to think about an issue before offering his opinion.

- Do not ever use the word "divorce." Once spoken it will always be out there.

- Do not bring up difficult conversations as soon as he walks through the door.

- Do not assume that you know what he is thinking.

- Do not take everything he says literally. He often uses jokes as a way to deal with things.

- Do not treat him like a child.

- Never talk about your sex life with anyone else.

- Do not expect him to be like your father or do what he would do.

- Do not withdraw from him when he touches you.

- Do not ever be alone with another man in a private setting.

- If you have a problem with him talk to him not someone else.

- Do not withhold sex as a way to punish him.

- Join him in the things he likes to pursue.

- Be sexy for him. He wants to be turned on by you. Tease him with your sexuality.

You will find it a bit more difficult to talk about this with a woman than with a man but it is good to teach this. When you do teach, the same principle for counseling a woman applies to pre-marital counseling. Never be alone and with the door closed. You can encourage future brides to speak to an older wiser woman in their lives.

Appendix E
Wedding Information

A successful wedding is in the details. The worksheet that follows these explanations will help you address many of those details. You will probably add others throughout your career.

Names. Get spelling and pronunciation correct. If you are not certain how to pronounce a name write it phonetically in your notes. Ask how they want you to refer to them, e.g. Robert or Bob?

Attendants. If a flower girl and/or ring bearer are very young, discuss the likelihood of the child getting stage fright and not doing what is planned. Make sure they realize that making a fuss over what a child does or does not do will distract from the wedding. Discuss what ushers will do. Ask who will hold the rings prior to the ring exchange.

Music. Talk about what instruments you have or allow and who will play. If using CDs, discuss how to make it quick and easy for the sound technician to switch from one song to another. If there will be a singer, discuss microphone and music stand needs.

Parents. These questions seem unnecessary, but if parents are divorced and do not get along, it will affect the rehearsal and wedding. Some divorced couples will not sit comfortably in the same row. Be ready to work this out.

Giving of the bride. Do you ask, "Who gives this woman to be married to this man?" or "Who presents this woman...?" or some other variant?

Elements in the ceremony. A homily is not required for a wedding, however it is an opportunity for you to teach about marriage. It is good to discuss your message with the couple privately, beforehand, as they will not "hear" much of it during the wedding itself.

If they are using an aisle runner you may need to tell them how long the aisle is. Also, discuss who will put the runner down and when.

Make sure you have a good understanding of how the wedding party will ingress and egress the venue and how they will be standing. The bride and groom should determine this.

Many couples continue the tradition that the groom and bride do not see each other prior to the ceremony. If so, you will have to discuss how to accomplish this.

After the ceremony. Most venues no longer allow throwing rice because it is too messy and difficult to clean, especially if it is raining. Birdseed is often used but it too is messy and drags into the building when taking pictures. Bubbles are a common alternative however, if people open them too early they may get spilled and create a spot on the carpet. I ask that they to be distributed only when guests are exiting the building.

** I do not attend receptions or rehearsal dinners unless my friendship with the couple would normally have my wife and me as guests.

** We require the couple to hire our sound technician to operate our sound system during rehearsal and wedding.

This form helps me cover all the fundamental things that go into a wedding.

Names:

Groom

Bride

Is she taking his last name?

Attendants:

How many women?

How many men?

Flower girl. Age?

Ring bearer. Age?

Ushers? How many?

Music:

Pianist/Organist

Guitar

CDs

Singer

How many songs?

Parents:

His: Are they together? Do they get along?

Hers: Are they together? Do they get along?

Who will escort the bride down the aisle?

Giving of the bride:

    Who will do this?

    Traditional or elsewise?

Elements in the ceremony:

    Roses for mothers

    Unity Candle

    Sand ceremony

    Communion

    Homily

    Aisle runner

    How will attendants enter?

        Men first?

        As pairs?

    How will attendants stand?

        Men and women on either side of couple?

        Stand as pairs?

    May groom see bride prior to the ceremony?

After the ceremony:

    Rice? Birdseed? Bubbles?

Appendix F
Wedding Homilies

Finding what you should say in a wedding homily can be taxing. You do not have to "reinvent the wheel." These sample messages can serve as a starting point for the homilies you develop. Use them as templates if you wish or use an entire message. I don't care if you credit me but if you use them, make them your own. Write them the way you would speak.[92]

Example One:

Like Everything Depends on You

On October 3, 2009 in Afghanistan, Clinton Romesha earned a Congressional Medal of Honor at the Battle of Command Outpost Keating, the most remote American base in that theater of war. Staff Sergeant Romesha led Red Platoon in a twelve hour battle against over 300 Taliban fighters.

In 2016 Romesha published a book detailing that battle and his actions throughout the fight.[93] His Medal of Honor citation reveals that the account in the book is not fiction. It's an exciting read that really caused me to think about the kind of soldier who earns an MOA. While they suffered 14 killed–in–action, the rest of the outpost survived in no small part because of the actions of SSG Romesha.

Certainly other soldiers could have been awarded an MOA from that battle. The reason anyone survived is that each man fought like everything depended on him. They each trusted the others to do the same. Romesha did what he had to do to protect everyone else in the platoon not thinking of his own life. He fought to win for every man at Outpost Keating. That's how you win at war.

---

92 These messages were written for specific couples and were intended for a listening audience, not readers of a book, so they may sound odd at times.

93 Romesha, *Red Platoon.*

Dick and Jane, you're about to go to war. (Y'all can enter jokes and wisecracks here.) All joking aside, marriage is a war in that there are many enemies ready to destroy a marriage. Entertainment and media seem to actually discourage fidelity in marriage. They promote a much different view of marriage than what God designed. There are people in your life who will, intentionally or not, create issues that test you. Financial circumstances may create anxiety. Even your families can cause unwanted stress. Now add things like a pandemic and the pressure of lock down and social distancing and we have a perfect storm for failed marriages. I'm not trying to discourage you. I want you to think about what you face and know that you can win this war. Many couples have done it.

The surest way to survive and thrive is for each of you to live as if it all depends on you. Dick, I challenge you to live as if the success of your marriage depends on you alone. Jane, I challenge you the same. It will not serve your marriage for either of you to look out primarily for yourself. Rather you both should live as if the success of your marriage all depends on you.

In my years of counseling couples who were struggling, one consistent factor I've seen is that one or both of a couple thinks that he or she is giving more than getting. When that starts, it's followed by one or both withholding love and service from the other in order to protect him/herself. To win this war against marriage, you need to think like Clinton Romesha. You can't control if your mate is doing his or her part. What matters is that you are doing all that you can to win. When you're both giving it your all, you will absolutely win.

That's what God intended for marriage. It's what He planned when He created men and women. God's Word says, *"Submit to one another out of reverence for Christ."*[94] The *"out of reverence for Christ"* part relates the command to God's plan. Submit to each other as God intended.

---

94 Ephesians 5:21

The Apostle wrote to both husbands and wives. He wrote to wives first. I want you to see that there is no verb in verse 22. The idea of submit carries over from verse 21. Here it merely says, *"Wives, to your husbands as to the Lord."*[95] He returns to the verb in verse 24 saying, *"wives should submit to their husbands in everything."*[96] This isn't about being a mousy doormat. It's about choosing to respect him as leader of the household. Jane, when you choose to submit to Dick you're living as if everything in your marriage depends on you. You're doing what you must in order for your marriage to be what both God and you want it to be. By submitting to your husband you're not thinking of yourself. You're fighting for your marriage.

Dick I'm sure you're familiar with verses 25–27, *"Husbands, love your wives, just as Christ loved the church and gave himself up for her to make her holy . . . to present her to Himself as a radiant church, without stain or wrinkle or any other blemish, but holy and blameless."*[97] Jesus loved the church so unselfishly that He was willing to sacrifice His life. He willingly did what was necessary to win, as if everything depended on Him. In fact everything did depend on Him. Jesus did it to present Christians holy before His Father; pure and blameless, perfectly without flaws. *That's* how you submit to Jane, by loving her, sacrificing yourself for her, loving and serving her as if your whole marriage depends on you. Live in a way that everyone who knows you as a couple sees that she is pure and blameless, without flaw in your eyes. Live as if your happiness and contentment is totally up to how you act.

You two will have to discover what this means in practical terms. I'm not going to give you a list of behaviors. You're smart enough to figure it out. I encourage you to approach your marriage from this perspective, each of you living as if everything depends on you.

---

95   Ephesians 5:22
96   Ephesians 5:24
97   Ephesians 5:25–27

Here's why this works. It only takes one of you to mess up the relationship. On the other hand, if you're both committed to doing what you must to win this war, you'll discover that marriage is the greatest gift God has given us on earth.

Example Two:

A Firm Foundation

Dick and Jane, I want to talk to you about the Brooklyn Bridge, not that I'm planning to sell it to you — unless you're interested in buying. Then I've got a deal for you. Actually I want to talk about the bridge itself. Construction began in 1869 and the bridge opened in 1883. It's a steel wire suspension design spanning 1595 feet connecting New York City with Brooklyn. There was a great controversy during construction, other than that the designer, John Augustus Roebling got his foot crushed by a ferry while surveying the project and died of tetanus infection.

In the early years of construction people of New York were upset that while the tower on the Brooklyn side stood 100 feet above the water, there seemed to be no work on the Manhattan side. In fact the New York tower was still 78 feet beneath the water and unseen to the citizens. The chief engineer wrote something like the following, I believe through a New York newspaper, *To such of the general public as might imagine that no work had been done on the New York tower, because they see no evidence of it above the water, I should simply remark that the amount of the masonry and concrete laid on that foundation during the past winter, under water, is equal in quantity to the entire masonry of the Brooklyn tower visible today above the waterline.* What people didn't realize is that the most difficult and daring work of building that foundation was done where no one could see it.

Gordon MacDonald used that story in his book *Building Below the Waterline*[98] to illustrate the principle that most of what Godly leaders do in their own lives and in the lives of others is done in the

98 MacDonald, *Building Below the Waterline.*

unseen quiet. I want to use it to illustrate a similar principle for a Godly marriage. Most of the work of building a Godly marriage is done out of the eye of family and friends and fellow church members.

Dick, I know that in your line of work you understand the importance of foundations. Every project begins with a proper foundation. Construct the foundation deep and strong and square and there's a good chance your building will stand. But if the foundation is weak or shallow or crooked, your building will be susceptible to a short lifespan, and it probably won't work right throughout its life.

This is absolutely true of marriage. One of the most common mistakes I see couples make is to think that they're going to be good at being married because they're in love. I wish it were true, but it's not. Many couples put great effort into their wedding, but not so much into the foundation of their marriage. Because they haven't established a proper foundation, when the novelty of being married wears off, which usually takes only a few years, they discover that there are cracks and weaknesses. Those cracks and weaknesses can lead to discord and brokenness and ultimately to collapse. We've all witnessed it.

I want to encourage you to work at building your foundation throughout your lives. Most of the work will be unseen by me and our church and even your family. It'll take place in the unseen quiet of your individual spiritual lives and in the things you do as a couple to give Jesus a central role in your relationship. Do the work.

Dick and Jane, you've begun well. I see your commitment to the church and to our Lord. I see your promises to each other. I am honored to listen to the vows you're going to promise to each other today. Think about this, being married is fun. Especially in the beginning, it's fun to have the one you love in your home. It's fun to share your experiences. It's fun to go through life together. After a while you'll get used to it. That's when many couples will begin to take it for granted, assuming that everything is always OK.

I want you to think about the things you're doing right now to build the foundation of your marriage. Don't ever stop doing these things. Don't ever let yourself think that you're good enough at relationship. Pay attention to your marriage. Always work on your foundation. Continue courting each other. Right now you're conscious of serving each other, of seeking to bless each other, of giving your all to each other. Don't ever stop. Everything else in your marriage will work right if you pay attention to your foundation. Throughout your lives together, always work on the foundation of your marriage and you'll enjoy marriage as God intended for you.

You've already made your promises to each other. You're about to make your promises before God and all of us. We rejoice with you. We pray for you. And we cheer for you. When you follow through on these promises not only will you be a blessing to each other, your marriage will be a blessing to the other people in your lives. And if God should one day give you children, you'll model for them what God intended for marriage to be.

Example Three:

Invest in Each Other

In the lobby of our church in La Porte, we have a plaque with the names of couples who have enjoyed fifty or more years of marriage. There are currently thirteen couples identified and more will be added soon. We have quite a few couples in our church with thirty–five plus years of marriage. Long and happy marriages don't happen by accident.

We all know that many marriages fail well before celebrating even twenty years. Many don't make it into double digits. Last year 2.14 million marriages were reported in the United States. Over 800,000 divorces were also reported. Nobody plans to divorce. When you exchange vows today you promise to love *until death do you part*, and I know you mean it. You desire a lifetime of love and joy. You're not thinking of ever drifting apart. You can't imagine that one day your hearts may be broken. You intend and expect to grow old together. The desire to love someone for a lifetime is God–given, the ability to so love requires that you love the other more than you love yourself.

A great marriage isn't the result of marrying the right person. It's the result of being the right person. Your love for each other has more to do with you than it does with the one you love. No one has enough personal magnetism to hold your love for the rest of your life. Dick, no matter how many great qualities Jane has, no matter how much you appreciate her, she cannot cause you to love her deeply. Jane, no matter how well Dick treats you, no matter how thoughtful and self–less he is, he cannot create your love for him.

Why do some marriages grow deep while others grow apart? Very simply, some couples invest in each other while some invest mostly in themselves. You've probably heard this axiom from the Bible, *"Where your treasure is, there your heart will be also."*[99] Our hearts and our treasures are linked. Treasure isn't just money or possessions of course. It's whatever you invest yourselves in. I encourage you to invest in each other.

My daughter has a dog that she absolutely loves. We don't know her breed. She's just a stray mutt and a little bit crazy. When she first showed up Bethany and Levi tried to find an owner of a missing a dog, but she seemed to be unwanted. She's fearful of being harmed and needy of attention. There's nothing special about her, but Bethany loves her. Bella didn't do anything to make Bethany love her. Bethany did. She invested herself in that little dog, feeding it and caring for it.

My other daughter, Rachel, when she birthed her first baby, endured several weeks of feeling lousy, morning sickness, sore back, fatigue. Eventually she went through a C–section. A nurse handed her the baby, she held him, and immediately fell in love with that little guy who had caused so much discomfort. She took him home

---

99   Matthew 6:21

and endured sleepless nights, noisy crying, messy diapers, and the hassle of carrying him and a bag of supplies everywhere she went. All the while, instead of getting tired of it, her love grew. Why? Because she invested herself in her son. If you meet a mother who isn't loving to her children, you can be sure she hasn't invested much of herself in them. Where there is little investment there is little love.

Your love will grow if you invest yourself in each other. If your love isn't growing, and especially if it's failing, you know you're not investing. Where there is little investment there is little love. The strength of your marriage and the depth of your love will be a direct consequence of your investment.

In your vows you'll promise that you will love completely and absolutely. You will keep that promise by investing yourself in the one you love. Earlier we heard two readings. One from the Bible, Romans 12:9–18, describes what real love looks like. I would encourage you to make those verses the theme of your marriage. Put them on a plaque or a poster. Type them and put them on your refrigerator. Read them often. Consider how each element applies to you and the one you love. The second reading, wisely chosen, reflects on what your vows mean. It talks about how you will treat each other, how you intend to look out for each other, how much of yourselves you intend to give to the other.

I think it's interesting, and probably intentional, that there's nothing in there about limits. The word *"unless"* isn't used. In your vows, you won't use the word "unless". You put no limits on your love. You make no qualifications on when or what you will invest in the other. Your vows are not a transaction. You won't say, *"I'll love you if"*. Your vows are a promise, *"I will love you no matter what."*

That's much different than a marriage in which everything is OK as long as they each get what they want out of it. Great marriages happen when a man invests himself in his wife and a woman invests herself in her husband. This is your promise today.

"Where your treasure is, there your heart will be also." Invest the best of yourself and all of yourself in each other. When you do you *will* enjoy a long love–filled marriage. If you're ready to make this promise of investing yourselves, will you now face each other and join hands to exchange your vows?

Example Four:

Fundamentals for a Successful Marriage

Jane, I'm going to use your connection to sports to make a point about marriage. As a coach you probably emphasize to your players that athletic greatness is more than natural talent. To be really good requires that a player learn and practice the fundamentals of the game. Great players practice the fundamentals; also, they practice the right fundamentals. Most coaches I know tell their players, *"Do the fundamentals well and the rest of the game will take care of itself."* Then they teach the right fundamentals to practice.

Have you ever had a teammate who was truly gifted but didn't work at her sport? Perhaps she started out noticeably better than most, but because she didn't work at it, eventually everybody else caught up and she was no longer that special player. You always have to work at the right fundamentals. That's true in every discipline of life. It's true of the building trades. It's true of learning to play a musical instrument. It's true of growing a vegetable garden. And it's true of marriage. Some people are naturally good at relationships. They seem to be made for marriage, but even they, if they don't pay attention to the fundamentals, are bound to fail. Just like those who succeed in sports, people who enjoy successful marriage, are the ones who pay attention to the fundamentals of relationships.

So let's think about some marriage fundamentals that if you work at these, I'm confident that you'll enjoy a great marriage. Here's the first one, *love*. Now I know your first response is, *"Well duh. That's why we're getting married. We're in love."* True enough, probably every marriage begins in love. The problem isn't the lack of love. The problem is that many couples don't work at it after they say *"I do."* Love is much more than good feelings. Love is a decision to put someone else first in your life.

Dick, to love Jane means that if necessary, you're willing to sacrifice your own pleasure to be a blessing to her. It means that taking care of her needs is more important to you than taking care of your own needs. Love means that her joy and comfort comes before your joy and comfort, and your will.

I often ask men something like this, *"If someone tried to harm your wife, would you give your life to protect her?"* Of course every man answers, *"Yes."* Then I point out that actually, the greatest threat to her happiness is you. Now Dick, you'll probably never have to die for Jane, so I encourage you to live for her. Make it your number one goal in life to bless Jane in everything. That's love.

Jane, you understand of course that the same is true for you. If you'll love Dick the way I just described, you'll both enjoy life beyond what you can imagine. And you'll enjoy success in marriage that even fairy tales can't compare.

The first fundamental for successful marriage is love. The second is *honesty*. No marriage will survive without honesty. Honesty has to do with what and how you communicate. Whether it's your spoken word or what you communicate in your behavior, your mate has to know the truth. That means you never lie or distort. There's no such thing as a "white lie." Honesty means you don't use half–truths to hide reality. Any dishonesty will hurt your relationship. Honesty also means that you share the events of your life. To keep something to yourself is to deprive your mate of part of you. So practice complete honesty.

Part of honesty in relationship is trust. Trust is receiving honesty from the other. Honesty will soon be lost if it's not rewarded by being received. Every man wants his wife to trust him. Every woman wants her husband's trust. Trust encourages openness. It communicates that you love your mate for who he/she is. Trust says, *"I accept you for who you are."* Trust gives you security to do your own thing because you know your honesty will be rewarded by your mate. Trust is tricky because it's so easily broken. Once broken it's very difficult to rebuild.

The opposite of trust is suspicion. Suspicion will fragment your relationship. Honesty and trust working hand in hand will keep your relationship secure. Honesty and trust may seem automatic, but they're not. You have to consciously work at them.

A third fundamental is *dependability*. Dependability is honesty in action. Dependability regards your promises, spoken and unspoken. It means you do what you say you're going to do. It means you fulfill your mate's reasonable expectations of you.

You can't depend on much in the world. Advertisers use you but they don't love you. Friends disappoint you. Governments lie to you. Your spouse needs dependability from you. Dependability requires that you make your promises wisely, realistically, according to your true abilities and your spouse's real needs. It requires that you remember your specific promises and your general marriage responsibilities. And it requires that you make being dependable a priority of your life.

A problem I see much too often goes like this: a crisis of some sort assails a relationship and one or the other decides that he/she needs out of the relationship. Precisely when the promise is needed, one or the other defaults on the promise saying, *"I didn't know it would be like this."* Of course not. That's the purpose of your vows, to assure stability in spite of the uncertain future and changing circumstances.

To be dependable you may have to sacrifice some unforeseen opportunity or deny yourself some personal advantage. It means you have to control the day without being moved by current events, continuing your love according to your vows and expectations. Think about this: If you're dependable in even small things, your spouse will be inspired to trust you in all things. That's quite a return for a simple investment.

One more fundamental that you should work at is *unselfishness*. Our natural tendency is to look out for ourselves. This is especially true in relationships. We seek to protect our interests and our likes. Unselfishness is one of the best keys to a happy marriage. If you bless the one you love you bless yourself. By unselfishly seeking what is best for your mate before yourself, you actually find what's best for yourself because after today you are no longer just Dick, and Jane. You're now Dick and Jane.

You are one. You're part of each other. What blesses one blesses the other, and that's more important than either of you as individuals. Unselfishness is the ability to surrender yourself for the sake of your marriage. It's the ability to put the concerns of your family before your individual concerns. So I encourage you to work at unselfishness for the sake of your marriage.

I once heard former Notre Dame Football coach Brian Kelly say that what makes a great football player is one who does ordinary things extraordinarily well. Let me say, what makes a great marriage is when a couple does the ordinary fundamental things extraordinarily well.

Why do some couples make it while some don't? It's because some couples work at the fundamentals while others assume that they'll survive on their natural charm and good feelings when they got married. If you'll attend to these fundamentals you will enjoy all the joy and success that God intends for marriage. It's your choice.

My prayer is that you will get these fundamentals right. You will be blessed. All of us here today, your friends and family, pray and hope that you will enjoy that wonderful life together.

Example Five:

How to Have a Perfect Marriage

That title suggests a lofty goal. Is there such a thing as a perfect marriage? And if there is, who am I to tell anybody else how to do it? Well I believe a perfect marriage is possible if you follow God's plan for husbands and wives. And I believe I'm the guy to tell you about it because I'm the guy you asked. So here are my thoughts.

Before we consider what can make a perfect marriage I want to describe three common mindsets that conflict with God's guidance. If you eliminate them you'll find it's easier to do marriage God's way.

One such mindset is *convenience*. We live in a world where personal convenience is highly valued. For example, even considering all the negatives associated with plastic, when was the last time you knew anybody who used cloth diapers? Disposable utensils and dishes are more convenient. We like instant credit, fast food, and drive through pick up. Convenience isn't bad, still I urge you to be careful. Do not let convenience control your decisions. Life isn't always convenient.

Because you're two different people some things in your lives will be inconvenient. If you approach marriage with the idea that everything should be convenient, you're going to be disappointed. Couples who have a convenience mindset find it easier to break the marriage than to deal with difficult issues together. Essentially, for some couples marriage is disposable. Don't think convenience!

Another harmful mindset is *individualism*. Individualism is the American way. You have individual rights. You have a right to be happy. Even when married you're still two individuals. Yes you are individuals, but you are forever linked as one. If you think as individuals you might look out for yourselves at the expense of the one you love. You might insist on having things your way. You might approach marriage thinking, *"What's in it for me?"* Individualism leads to competing instead of cooperating, pursuing selfish interests

189

instead of building each other up, living with individual priorities and agendas instead of living as one. A mindset of individualism will hurt your marriage.

A third deadly mindset is *distrust*. It's easy to become cynical as we get used to people not living up to what they say. Politicians tell us what they think we want to hear. Journalists slant their stories. Advertisers are just honest enough to not get sued.

Absolute honesty isn't even expected anymore. When someone is caught in a lie he is excused because he merely "misspoke." Your marriage cannot survive distrust. You must trust and be trustworthy. If you bring distrust into your marriage, as if you expect dishonesty from each other, you'll never be sure of your relationship.

This is why I emphasize your vows. You don't have to say any vows to get married. Legally all you have to do is agree to the contract and sign the papers. But that won't make a marriage. I encourage you to very carefully promise only what you intend to keep. A mindset of distrust will make your marriage vows meaningless.

The purpose of your vows is to assure each other that even if everything else changes, your love and commitment never will. In your vows today you'll offer no exceptions or qualifiers. You promise unending love and devotion.

A mindset of distrust will excuse failure, and it will destroy any relationship, especially a marriage. So then, what does God say about marriage? And it's not, *"Forgive them for they know not what they do!"*

I believe God's plan for a perfect marriage involves two mindsets. The first is *love*. I know that sounds like it goes without saying. Of course you're in love. That's why you're getting married. I'm not talking about love as it is so often mis–used in our culture. People mistake infatuation with love, or think that love means to really, really, really like someone. A mindset that can make a perfect marriage is love as God defined and demonstrated. We're all familiar with what is often called the love chapter where the Bible says, *"Love is patient, love is kind. It does not envy, it does not boast, it is not proud. It is not rude, it is not self–seeking, it is not easily angered, it keeps no record of wrongs. Love does not delight in evil but rejoices with the truth. It always protects, always trusts, always hopes, always perseveres."*[100]

I encourage you, don't just glance at that passage superficially. Read it carefully. Study each word. Then live up to that definition. If the things that love is describe you, and if you avoid the things that love is not, you're on your way to that perfect marriage.

The other mindset in God's plan is *submission*. The Apostle Paul wrote this about marriage, *"Submit to one another out of reverence for Christ."*[101] After that he wrote, *"Wives, to your husbands as to the Lord,"*[102] and *"Husbands love your wives just as Christ loved the church and gave Himself up for her."*[103] Similarly in Colossians Paul wrote, *"Wives, submit to your husbands, as is fitting in the Lord. Husbands, love your wives and do not be harsh with them."*[104] Peter also wrote about submission, *"Wives . . . be submissive to your husbands, and, Husbands . . . be considerate as you live with your wives, and treat them with respect."*[105]

Submission is rather a negative concept in our day but it wasn't to Paul and Peter. Submission isn't about weakness or subservience. It's not about becoming your spouse's footstool. Submission is about having the personal strength to willingly put your mate before yourself. It's about choosing to serve your wife or husband. It's about being a blessing to the one you love. If either of you is self-ish, if you take advantage of the other, submission will be painful. But if you each submit to one another, promoting what's best for the other, you'll both benefit and your marriage will grow closer and closer every day.

---

100 First Corinthians 13:4–7
101 Ephesians 5:21
102 Ephesians 5:22
103 Ephesians 5:25
104 Colossians 3:18–19
105 First Peter 3:1,7

A perfect marriage? Yes it's possible. Dick you can be that loving, serving husband. You can choose to bless Jane in everything. But you have to decide that's the kind of man you will be. Jane you can choose to serve and support Dick as he leads your family. If you bring into your marriage the mindsets of true Biblical love and submission, not only can you, but you *will* enjoy a perfect marriage.

I have observed how you are with each other. Your love is genuine. And I know you desire to be true Jesus followers. Your faithfulness is evident. Don't strive for convenience but for unity; learn to think as "Dick and Jane" and no longer Dick *or* Jane. And build on trust. Then follow God's guidance to love and serve, and you will enjoy a perfect marriage that will be a blessing to all the people in your lives.

Example Six:

Enjoy the Ordinary

Dick and Jane, you're about to begin a great adventure. I think being married is the second greatest experience on earth, second only to being saved. The day you get married is a time of great joy, but life is not all about great joyous moments. I want to encourage you, "Enjoy all the moments of your life together, the great moments and the common ones."

Someone once said *"great thanksgiving usually comes from great appreciation of common things rather than from a great supply of many things."* Let's think about that for a few moments because there's a lot of wisdom in it. I think many people miss some of the joy of life because they are looking for the great and spectacular instead of seeing treasure in the common.

Many couples will happily marry but then miss the blessing of marriage. They're in love, and they intend to be married until death do they part. They'll commit to live the rest of their lives as one but they'll miss the real blessing because they're looking for the wrong thing. The joy of marriage is found not in the exciting events that come our way periodically, but in the day–to–day events that are our lives.

It's easy to ignore these common experiences as just another day. They're not common because you live those moments together. You get to be present to rejoice in the ups and share the burden of each other's downs. Those common days become special when you see them as treasures in which you have shared each other's lives, you carried each other's burdens, comforted each other's grieving, encouraged each other's laughter, and built up each other's strengths.

Listen to me carefully, *"If you look for joy only in the spectacular events, you'll miss the real joy of life together."* The joy of marriage comes in sharing the common. Every experience is another treasure to be enjoyed in its commonness.

The Bible teaches us that a husband and wife become one through their love as they submit to each other. I find it interesting that there's no mention of spectacular events bringing about the unity of husband and wife. It's really quite simple, a husband loves his wife, putting her needs and concerns above even his own, and a wife respects and honors her husband. This is the nature of the marriage relationship as God planned it, each of you giving all of yourself to bless the other.

Dick, if you allow, God will work to mold you into the kind of husband Jane needs. He already knows exactly what she needs from you in order for her to be what He wants. God is prepared to make you into that man. If you follow Him you will be a blessing to her. Sadly too many husbands look to their wives not as someone to bless but as someone to use for their own goals. Don't do it. Always remember that you are her husband so that God can work through you to bring her closer to Christ.

Jane, if you'll give yourself to Dick as the Bible teaches, God will work in both of you. Don't be afraid of the Biblical concept of submission. Tony Evans once said about submission something like,

For a wife to submit to her husband simply means that she should duck so that God can hit her husband. Unfortunately, many wives actually get in the way of God's work when they try to control their husbands. I encourage you, be the wife Dick needs and let God make him the husband you need.

In a few minutes you're going to publicly declare your commitment to each other. You'll state your determination to become one and remain one for the rest of your lives. I haven't seen your vows yet so let me ask you both: Have you included any limitations on your love and commitment? For example a maximum number of years? Do you include a caveat that if life gets tough your promise is no longer valid? Is there anything about dropping the whole thing if you get bored? Do you include an escape clause in case one of you gets sick, or if you're struggling to get along? Of course not. You're thinking, *"'till death do us part"*, as you should.

When you're getting along, when you're connecting, you'll love being together, you'll talk easily and laugh freely. You'll touch each other naturally and lovingly. You'll encourage each other and celebrate each other's uniqueness. You'll serve each other joyfully and tease each other playfully. This is love. This is the unity, the oneness God intends for marriage.

But what happens when you hit a crisis? You're going to discover that there'll be times when you disconnect. Sin, temperamental differences, exhaustion, outside pressures, the demands of life, even family can put pressure on your relationship. At times like these, you may panic, thinking that a temporary disconnect signals disaster. Not so!

The promise you make today, your wedding vow is a commitment to get through those times, to do the work of reconciliation when necessary. Your promise will get you over temporary disconnection. You're not headed for ruin but it all depends on the integrity of your word.

That should make a great difference for you. Disconnection is not a precursor of disaster. Instead of focusing on the trouble, remember your promise. In spite of any difficulty you might face, you have a rock–solid commitment to each other that'll see you through the moments of disconnection and back into oneness.

I say again, appreciate even the episodes of disconnection, not because conflict is a good thing, but because in them God is teaching you and strengthening you. Right now all is well. You're ready to begin married life with someone you love with your whole being. You have so many good things to enjoy. But what will the future bring?

We used to have a woman in our church who seldom came to church, and I was and am so proud of her. You see her husband suffered from Alzheimer's disease. I would have been disappointed in her if she came to church because she had promised to be there for him in sickness and in health. As long as he was alive, she kept her promise. She attended to him every day. She got him up in the morning and fed him breakfast. She stayed with him throughout the day, then put him to bed each night. She did this every day without a break or vacation until the day God called him home.

She shared with me the prayer she prayed every day: *When I no longer have what I now enjoy, may God give me the grace to enjoy what I then shall have.* That wasn't the life she envisioned when she married Terry, but to her it was an opportunity to demonstrate her love in a way that few people ever will.

Enjoy what you have every day asking God to help you. Your lives will change as the years go by. Most of your experiences will be ordinary, common, everyday things that you might view as mundane. Enjoy them as treasures. God has blessed you. Make the most of that blessing.

Example Seven:

The Love of Your Lifetime

Read Matthew 19:3-6; Ephesians 5:19-33

What a wonderful day this is. Nothing can take away the significance and joy of this occasion. In the spirit of the old U.S. Postal Service motto, *Neither rain nor heat nor wind nor lightning and thunder shall keep us from this celebration of love,* although right about now the cool of a little snow would feel good. Today is about celebrating your covenant of marriage, and nothing is going to distract from our joy.

Entering into this covenant is both exciting and scary. It's exciting because you're about to change your lives forever. It's scary because both the concept and definition of marriage has been seriously jacked up in our society over the past few decades and you're probably not sure what to expect. Nevertheless, we will not be deterred from following God's plan. In the passage from Matthew is a most important teaching from Jesus about God's intention for marriage, one man, one woman, one flesh.

There was a time when marriages were arranged by parents. In that case perhaps it was necessary to *remind* a couple of God's intent. A man had not necessarily chosen his wife. She was chosen for him whether or not he loved her. A woman didn't choose her husband. Her parents chose him for any number of reasons, the least of which was her love for him.

Times have changed. Now we choose our own mates. You have chosen each other. Dick you chose Jane because you love her. Jane you chose Dick for that same love. You have chosen each other in full knowledge of God's plan: *One man, one woman, uniting to become one flesh.* I commend you for your choice. That sounds pretty good, truly it's a recipe for the love of your lifetime, a lifelong marriage of joy and happiness. And I'm confident that you can enjoy just such a marriage. The question is never, "*Can* you do it?" The question

196

is, *"Will* you do it?" No one can do it for you. No one can arrange a happy joyful marriage for you. *You* will either create a happy joy–filled marriage or you will create something else.

Today you become a statistic. You are one of about 46,000 couples who will get married in Ohio in 2017. You are one of 18,000 of your age who marry in 2017. You become one of 2.9 million married couples in the state of Ohio. I have another question for you. *How will you avoid being part of this next statistic?* Statistically, about twelve percent of couples in Ohio will fail to be true to God's design for the marriage covenant. How will you beat that statistic?

A mistake that many couples make is to think that because they're in love, love will find a way. Not necessarily, in fact for one in ten couples it doesn't. You have to make a way. You have to make this covenant become the love of your lifetime. Dick and Jane, you have everything you need to be *one man, one woman, one flesh,* but you have to make it happen. How will you make sure that the love you have right now doesn't fail?

You already know the answer. That's why you asked for a reading of Ephesians 5. What was read is a fair translation, but I want you to hear and remember some insights from the original text. Paul began a thought in verse 18 about being filled with the Spirit. In verses 19–20 he wrote that we express the Holy Spirit in our lives by, *"singing and making music in our hearts to the Lord, always giving thanks to God the Father."* [106]

Our English translations usually turn verse 21 into an imperative, a command, *submit to one another.* But the verb is actually a participle and should be translated, *"submitting to one another out of reverence for Christ."*[107] The Apostle isn't commanding, he's explaining that we give thanks to God when we submit to one another. We give thanks by following his plan for relationships.

106 Ephesians 5:19–20
107 Ephesians 5:21

Starting in verse 21 he applies his thoughts to specific categories of relationships. For our purpose today we're looking at just one, the husband/wife relationship. Paul didn't actually instruct wives to submit to their husbands. The thought carries over from verse 21 as he advised wives how to relate to their husbands. God's plan is that wives who humbly submit to their husbands as to the Lord are giving thanks to God. He based this on God's plan that husbands are intended to serve as head of the "one flesh" just as Christ is the head of the one church.

There's nothing demeaning in this. It's not a forced relationship. It's a choice a wife makes to honor God's plan for marriage. Jane, I encourage you to choose to submit to Dick's leadership. Trust him to lead as a man of God. I am confident that when you follow God's plan your marriage will be blessed.

I think it's interesting that the only imperative, or command in this scripture is to husbands. *"Husbands, love your wives, just as Christ loved the church."*[108] God commands husbands to love their wives probably because we are more likely than our wives to be selfish and self-concerned. Whatever the reason, a man of God doesn't have a choice. He must love his wife regardless of any return. When a husband leads in love, his wife almost always follows.

The nature of that love is unselfish, sacrificial, and unconditional, the same way Jesus loved the church. Jesus ceded the splendor of Heaven for the sake of his bride. He willingly accepted terrible suffering and even death for the sake of his bride. That's the kind of love God intends for a husband as he submits to his wife. Dick, God is telling you that whatever the cost to you, your love should make Jane's life beautiful, free from any doubt about your love; free from the pain of broken relationship; and shining with the joy of being loved absolutely. God's plan is that your love will be the greatest of blessings for her.

---

108 Ephesians 5:25

I asked you earlier, how will you make this happen? How will you make sure your marriage is not only the love of your lifetime, but is joy–filled and happy? I have a simple suggestion. Be intentional about your love. What I mean is, think and plan how you will communicate and demonstrate your love. Learn to say *"I love you."* Every person has a particular language of love. If you learn each other's love language, communicating your love will be sure and easy. It won't happen automatically. You must make it happen.

You also have to show your love. Some couples say *"I love you"* but their behavior betrays something less than love. In long–lasting joy–filled marriages both husband and wife are intentional about communicating and demonstrating their love. In your marriage vows you're going to promise this very love, and you'll promise it until you are parted by death. Every couple promises that, but not every couple does it. There are too many distractions and hindrances even for love to last without effort. You can do it if you're intentional about it. Isn't that the purpose of the vow? You promise that you intend to keep your love alive. Whatever may come, your love will continue. It's up to you to do what you promise. I assure you, if you live up to your vow, your love and marriage will last your lifetime.

I encourage you to be intentional about saying *"I love you"* and about demonstrating your love. My prayer for you is that the love you have today is the least your love will ever be. If you're ready to make that commitment official and legal, will you face each other, join hands, and speak your vows?

Example Eight:

Seven Steps to a Great Marriage

You're going to get a lot of advice from friends and family about what to expect and how to enjoy your marriage. Over the years I've gathered a *"Top Ten"* list of the advice that people have shared with couples:

Ten: The husband who wants a happy marriage should learn to keep his mouth shut and his checkbook open.

Nine: Marriage is an opportunity for a man to find out what kind of man his wife would have preferred.

Eight: You shouldn't marry for money; you can borrow it cheaper.

Seven: A man should marry only a very pretty woman in case he should ever want some other man to take her off his hands.

Six: Most men are brainless, so a woman might have to try more than one to find a live one.

Five: If you're arguing with your wife, never get out of the car.

The rest of these are from young children:

Four: You should marry somebody who likes the same stuff. Like if you like sports, she should like it that you like sports, and she should keep the chips and dip coming.

Three: It's better for girls to be single but not for boys. Boys need somebody to clean up after them!

Two: No person really decides before they grow up who they're going to marry. God decides it all way before, and you get to find out later who you're stuck with."

One: Tell your wife that she looks pretty even if she looks like a truck!

As I said, you can expect plenty of advice from well–meaning family and friends sometime during the reception. People will say nice things about you and offer their particular words of advice.

Usually the speaker will have some good thoughts to share, but almost everyone will tell you that difficult times are headed your way but if you work hard at it you can survive.

Now I suppose that's not all bad because most marriages do go through tough times. But it just seems to me that all the negative talk could discourage you. So I like to take a different tack. I believe marriage is just about the greatest experience on this earth, second only to being saved. I think you're in for a wonderful adventure and you don't have to fear the negative things that people like to warn about. So I'd like to offer some positive advice to help you make the most of your marriage.

You are about to exchange your vows, promises you make to each other. Your vows alone will not make your marriage happy and joyful. Happiness requires that you work at making it what it should be. I promise you, when you do it right, marriage is a blessing to you and everyone who is part of your lives.

My wife and I have been married for 46 plus years, and our marriage is still in process. The fact is that every marriage, every relationship is always in process. One benefit of that process is that you can do things to make it always better than it is now. Let me, very briefly, share seven steps you can take to move your marriage in the right direction.

Number One: If you have any past failures, deal with them. Everybody brings baggage with them when they enter a relationship and this is certainly true of marriage. Past failures will not, by themselves, destroy your marriage, but they can become a problem, especially if you've tried to keep something secret but it comes out. If you've made mistakes, confess them, then let them go. Don't let some past failure injure your current relationship.

Number Two: Develop and maintain a positive attitude. Attitude often makes the difference between a joyful and affirming marriage and a painful, discouraging one. A negative, critical attitude makes for a cold relationship whereas a positive attitude, which looks for what is best for your spouse, strengthens and affirms your relationship and leads to warmth.

Number Three: Discover the primary way your spouse says, "I Love You." I have a library of about 2300 books, most of which I have read. One of my favorites is entitled, *How Do You Say "I Love You"?* The author talks about the different ways that people express their love. Some people give gifts; some touch; some write love notes; others help with chores; some people say *"I love you"* by spending time together. Understand that each of you may say *"I love you"* differently. Learn how you say, *"I love you"*, and how your mate says, *"I love you."* Discover how your spouse expresses love and learn to hear *"I love you."* In this you create a climate in which you both flourish. Each of you, secure in love, will blossom and become all that God created you to be.

Number Four: Learn the art of empathetic listening. One of the most powerful tools you have to build your relationship is the ability to listen. Whenever your spouse is talking, listen carefully. Listen not only to his/her words, but also to feelings, thoughts, and desires. Hear what is not said. Through empathy you come to really understand your spouse, and that understanding helps you grow and become a better person.

Number Five: Discover the joy of helping your spouse succeed. You will find few accomplishments in life more satisfying or with greater results than helping your spouse accomplish the purposes for which God created him/her. Some couples discourage each other from progress or accomplishment because they're afraid they'll get left behind. Don't fear each other's success, but encourage and enable success and you'll both grow from it, and your relationship will be stronger as you share the rewards of success.

Number Six: Learn to enjoy your differences. God made you different for a purpose. He wants you to complement each other. Dick, you fulfill Jane's life, and Jane you fulfill Dick's. Your differences are assets to your relationship. In this you build each other up and help each other be what God created you to be. When you learn to enjoy your differences, you both become winners in life.

Number Seven: Make it a top priority to be a positive influence on your spouse. People often talk about how a marriage is a 50/50 thing where both of the couple compromise to make things work. I suggest that you determine to make it a 100/100 thing. Give 100% of yourself, regardless if your spouse does the same. You can't control your spouse's behavior, but you can always be a positive influence. Your positive influence may be just the thing he/she needs to give 100% also.

You have all the tools you need for a marriage of rich blessings and individual growth. Now it's up to you to make it happen. If you follow through with the promises of your vows, you'll experience that joy.

Example Nine:

When Does Your Marriage Begin?

After a lot of love and hard work by family and friends to get this place ready, here we are at what is perhaps the most significant moment of your life. In just a few moments, you're lives are going to change dramatically, from two individuals who happen to meet in the course of time, to a couple, committed and dedicated to each other for the rest of your lives on earth. So I want you to think about a question. "When does your marriage begin?"[109] That's an intriguing question. At what point in time do you change from being an engaged couple to being a married couple? If you know your answer to this question you will also know what it means to be married.

Many if not most people cannot offer a carefully thought through answer. One might answer something like, *"Marriage begins when our love becomes so strong we can no longer imagine being without,"*

---

109 This idea came from Walt Wangerin in his book As For Me and My House.

or, *"Marriage begins when we decide to live forever together and raise children."* A true romantic might answer, *"Marriage begins when our love is so deep we choose to be together for the rest of our lives."* Those are good and acceptable answers, but they fail to identify a precise moment in time when a couple moves from not married to married. Imagine the time line of your life as a line on paper that stretches miles long. Somewhere along that line is a point, a dot before which you were not married and after which you are married. To discover that point you will then also know what constitutes marriage; exactly what it means to be married.

So when does marriage begin? It must not be when you fall in love for there are many couples in love who are not married. It cannot be the first time a couple makes love for again there are many couples who engage in love–making but have made no commitment to each other. Marriage doesn't begin at engagement for engagement is in no way binding. A couple may just change their minds and go separate ways. Go online and see how many unused engagement rings are for sale. We may be saddened if our friends' engagement is called off, but we then think *"better now than after the wedding."*

Neither does living together equal marriage. Most people I've talked to about living together say that it is a time to discover if they have what it takes to get married but there is nothing permanent in living together. One good fight can and often does end it all.

Love is an extraordinary experience and often leads to marriage, but it is not marriage. Sex is a wonderful gift from our creator. It's fun. It draws two to become one. And it produces the children we want to raise, but it is not marriage. Living together is convenient and often saves living costs as a couple shares expenses, but without commitment there is nothing to assure that they will stay together, thus living together is not marriage.

So again, when does marriage begin? Did God or fate decide, leaving you no choice in the matter? I think not. You are responsible your marriage. I believe that there is a clear beginning to your marriage that can be identified that must be consistent with what marriage truly is. It is that moment in time when you move from being not married to being married. You decide to make that move. *You,* hopefully, with careful thought, aware of the implications, decide to be married.

I believe that moment is when you consciously make a clear, unqualified promise to be faithful and committed to each other for the rest of your lives. That's why we have wedding ceremonies. You make and receive promises. In that you moves your relationship from not married to married. That's the point in time that marriage begins. It's when you commit to each other all of yourselves for the rest of your lives. That's why what you say in your wedding vows is so important, because your lives together are built on that vow.

Marriage is not really built on your love. Your love enables and provokes you to keep your promise. Marriage isn't built on sex. Sex helps draw you to become one with each other. Marriage isn't living together. Actually living together often challenges marriage when two people aren't very good at putting someone else before themselves. Even believing that this is God's will doesn't make your marriage. Your promise makes your marriage. Your promise publically stated and willingly received creates the union we call marriage.

Two qualities of your vow changes your relationship into a marriage. One, is that it is *total*. In your vows you promise all of yourselves to each other. Not just some. Not even most. Everything you are and everything you have you commit to the other. You hold nothing back. The other important quality is that your promise is timeless. You promise until death do you part. Every wedding I have ever performed has included a phrase to that effect, "until we are parted by death" or "until God shall call us home."

There is no expiration date on your promise. You include no limitations, through sickness and health, for richer or poorer, through good times or bad.

Couples whose marriages fail almost always fail at keeping the vow. For whatever reason one or both of them has changed the conditions of the promise. *"I didn't think it would be like this." "I'm tired of the same old thing." "I'm not attracted to you anymore."* Isn't that the very reason you make a promise? Things will change, you will change. You promise that circumstances or changes won't undo your love and commitment. When storms and troubles come your way, while lesser marriages might not survive, yours will because of your promise.

From the moment you state your promise and receive a promise from your chosen mate, your marriage begins. Then it's up to you to keep your promise alive. No one can do it for you. You're responsible to live according to what you promise today. If you keep your promises, you will enjoy a wonderful lifelong marriage. If you fail at your promises, you'll experience heart–breaking turmoil. I'm confident that as mature adults you willingly and joyfully make this commitment. Your lives will change today because of the vow you will make. Your marriage will begin when you give and receive this promise.

Appendix G
Wedding Vows

Number One:

Dick, do you take this woman, whose hand you now hold, to be your wedded wife? Will you love her, honor her, cherish her, protect her, and keep yourself only to her so long as you both shall live? (Answer: "I do!")

Jane, do you take this man, whose hand you now hold, to be your wedded husband? Will you love him, honor him, cherish him, protect him, and keep yourself only to him so long as you both shall live? (Answer: "I do!")

Number Two:

Dick, do you take this woman, whose hand you now hold, to be your lawfully wedded wife? And do you promise before God and these witnesses that you will be to her a true and devoted husband; true to her in sickness and in health, in joy and in sorrow, in prosperity and in adversity, and that forsaking all others you will keep yourself to her, and to her only until God shall separate you by death? (Answer: "I do!")

Jane, do you take this man, whose hand you now hold, to be your lawfully wedded husband? And do you promise before God and these witnesses that you will be to him a true and devoted wife; true to him in sickness and in health, in joy and in sorrow, in prosperity and in adversity, and that forsaking all others you will keep yourself to him, and to him only, until God shall separate you by death? (Answer: "I do!")

Number Three:

Dick, will you take this woman to be your wedded wife, to live together after God's ordinance in holy matrimony? Will you love her, comfort her, honor her, and keep her in sickness and health, and forsaking all others, keep yourself only to her so long as you both shall live? (Answer: "I will!")

Jane, will you take this man to be your wedded husband, to live together after God's ordinance in holy matrimony? Will you love him, comfort him, honor him, and keep him in sickness and health, and forsaking all others, keep yourself only to him so long as you both shall live? (Answer: "I will!")

Number Four:

Dick do you solemnly agree before God and these witnesses to take this woman to be your lawful wedded wife, to love and respect her, honor and cherish her, in health and in sickness, in prosperity and in adversity, and leaving all others, to keep yourself only to her so long as you both shall live? (Answer: "I do!")

Jane, do you solemnly agree before God and these witnesses to take this man to be your lawful wedded husband, to love and respect him, honor and cherish him, in health and in sickness, in prosperity and in adversity, and leaving all others, to keep yourself only to him so long as you both shall live? (Answer: "I do!")

Number Five:

Dick, please repeat after me:

I, Dick, take you Jane, to be my wedded wife. And I do promise before God and these witnesses, to be your loving and faithful husband, in plenty and in want, in joy and in sorrow, in sickness and in health, so long as we both shall live.

Jane, please repeat after me:

I, Jane, take you Dick, to be my wedded husband. And I do promise before God and these witnesses, to be your loving and faithful wife, in plenty and in want, in joy and in sorrow, in sickness and in health, so long as we both shall live.

Number Six:

Dick, will you please repeat after me:

I, Dick, in the presence of God and these witnesses, promise to you, Jane, my love and protection. I promise to cherish you forever. As Christ so loved the church that He gave His life for her, I also give to you my fullest love. Jane, I promise to provide for you in health and in sickness, in times of plenty and in time of want. I promise to be true to you alone, joining with you until we are parted by death.

Jane, will you please repeat after me:

I, Jane, in the presence of God and these witnesses, promise to you, Dick, my love, honor, and faithfulness. I promise to cherish you forever. As the church is in subjection to Christ, so shall I be subject unto you in all matters. I promise to be your helper and partner throughout our lives together, until we are parted by death.

Number Seven:

Do you, Dick, take this woman to be your lawful wedded wife, to love and to cherish, to have and to hold, in sickness and in health, for better and for worse, forsaking all others until death do you part? (Answer: "I do!")

Do you, Jane, take this man to be your lawful wedded husband, to love and to cherish, to have and to hold, in sickness and in health, for better or for worse, forsaking all others until death do you part? (Answer: "I do!")

Number Eight:

Dick, please repeat after me:

I, Dick, take you Jane, to be my wedded wife. Let us share together from this day forward, in the good and the bad of life, in the strengths and weaknesses of life. I will cherish you, love you, and be friends with you, until death shall finally separate us. I now pledge my life and love to you.

Jane, please repeat after me:

I, Jane, take you Dick, to be my wedded husband. Let us share together from this day forward, in the good and the bad of life, in the strengths and weaknesses of life. I will cherish you, love you and be friends with you, until death shall finally separate us. I now pledge my life and love to you.

Number Nine:

Dick, do you take this woman to be your wedded wife, to live together after God's ordinance in the holy estate of matrimony? Do you promise to love her, comfort her, honor her, and keep yourself only to her as long as you both shall live? (Answer: "I do!")

Jane, do you take this man to be your wedded husband, to live together after God's ordinance in the holy estate of matrimony? Do you promise to love her, comfort her, honor her, and keep yourself only to her as long as you both shall live? (Answer: "I do!")

Dick, please repeat after me:

I, Dick, take you Jane, to be my wedded wife. Let us share together from this day forward, in the good and the bad in life, in the strengths and weaknesses of life. I will cherish you, love you, and be friends with you, until death shall finally separate us. I now pledge my life and love to you.

Jane, please repeat after me:

I, Jane, take you Dick, to be my wedded husband. Let us share together from this day forward, in the good and the bad of life, in the strengths and weaknesses of life. I will cherish you, love you, and be friends with you, until death shall finally separate us. I now pledge my life and love to you.

Number Ten:

Dick, will you take Jane to be your wedded wife? Will you share with her from this day forward, in the good and bad of life, in the strengths and weaknesses of life? Will you cherish her, love her, and be friends with her, until death shall finally separate you? Will you now pledge your life and love to her? (Answer: "I will!")

Jane, will you take Dick to be your wedded husband? Will you share with him from this day forward, in the good and bad of life, in the strengths and weaknesses of life? Will you cherish him, love him, and be friends with him, until death shall finally separate you? Will you now pledge your life and love to him? (Answer: "I will!")

Number Eleven:

Dick, will you take Jane to be your lawfully wedded wife, to live together after God's Holy ordinances in the Holy union of marriage? Will you love her, serve her, honor and cherish her, and forsaking all others, keep yourself only unto her as long as you both shall live? (Answer: "I will!")

Jane, will you take Dick to be your lawfully wedded husband, to live together after God's Holy ordinances in the Holy union of marriage? Will you love him, serve him, honor and cherish him, and forsaking all others, keep yourself only unto him as long as you both shall live? (Answer: "I will!")

Number Twelve:

Dick, will you have Jane to be your wedded wife, to live together in the holy estate of matrimony? Will you love her, comfort her, honor her, and keep her, in sickness and in health and forsaking all others keep yourself only to her so long as you both shall live? (Answer: "I will!")

Jane, will you have Dick to be your wedded husband, to live together in the holy estate of matrimony? Will you love him, comfort him, honor him, and keep him, in sickness and in health, and forsaking all others keep yourself only to him so long as you both shall live? (Answer: "I will!")

Dick, please repeat after me:

I, Dick, take you Jane, to be my wedded wife, to have and to hold, from this day forward, for better, for worse, for richer, for poorer, in sickness and in health, to love and to cherish, till death do us part.

Jane, please repeat after me:

I, Jane, take you Dick, to be my wedded husband, to have and to hold, from this day forward, for better, for worse, for richer, for poorer, in sickness and in health, to love and to cherish, till death do us part.

Number Thirteen:

Do you, Dick, in the presence of Almighty God and these witnesses here present, promise to love and cherish, and to protect this woman, Jane, whose hand you now hold? Do you promise to provide for her in health and in sickness? Do you promise to be true to her, forsaking all others, cleaving unto her and her only until death do you part? (Answer: "I do!")

Do you, Jane, in the presence of Almighty God and these witnesses here present, promise to love and to cherish, and to honor this man, Dick, whose hand you now hold? Do you promise to provide for him in health and in sickness? Do you promise to be true to him, forsaking all others, cleaving unto him and him only until death do you part? (Answer: "I do!")

Number Fourteen:

Dick, will you please repeat after me:

I, Dick, take you Jane, to be my wife. I commit my life to you, embracing all joys and sorrows, all triumphs and hardships. I promise to submit to Christ as leader of our home. I promise to serve you as Jesus teaches me to be a servant. And I pray that God will cause me to become the husband He's called me to be. I make this commitment in love. I keep it in faith. I live it in joy. With God as my witness and my strength, I pledge you my love.

Jane, will you please repeat after me:

I, Jane, take you Dick, to be my husband. I commit my life to you, embracing all joys and sorrows, all triumphs and hardships. I promise to submit to you as the church is in submission to Christ. I promise to serve you as Jesus teaches me to be a servant. And I pray that God will cause me to become the wife He's called me to be. I make this commitment in love. I keep it in faith. I live it in joy. With God as my witness and my strength, I pledge my love.

Appendix H
Ring Exchange

These rings symbolize the very essence of marriage. The circle is an emblem of eternity, a never ending love between a man and a woman. The precious metal symbolizes that which is least tarnished and most enduring. The rings are to remind us how lasting and imperishable the union between these two shall be.

Number One:

Dick, please repeat after me as you place this ring on the finger of your bride:

Jane, wear this ring as a symbol of my love for you. This ring symbolizes the unending union of my life with yours. Your dreams are now my dreams, your hopes are my hopes, your fears are my concerns, your affection is my joy, your love is my blessing.

Jane, please repeat after me as you place this ring on the finger of your groom:

Dick, wear this ring as a symbol of my love for you. This ring symbolizes the unending union of my life with yours. Your dreams are now my dreams, your hopes are my hopes, your fears are my concerns, your affection is my joy, and your love is my blessing.

Dick and Jane, in the years to come, as you look upon these rings, be reminded of the covenant that you made here today. Remember the promises of your vows and the joy that came with them. Remember also the oneness you feel right now. May these rings help keep you focused on each other as the most important person in the world to you.

Number Two:

Dick, please repeat after me as you place this ring on the finger of your bride: With this ring, I give you my heart this day, and promise to love you, for the rest of my life.

Jane, please repeat after me as you place this ring on the finger of your groom: With this ring, I give you my heart this day, and promise to love you, for the rest of my life.

By the speaking of your vows and the exchanging of these rings, you Dick and Jane, have committed your lives to each other. From this time on you shall be as one.

Number Three:

Dick, do you have a ring? As you place this ring on the finger of your bride, please repeat after me: This ring I give you in token and pledge of our constant faith and abiding love.

Jane, do you have a ring? As you place this ring on the finger of your groom, please repeat after me: This ring I give you in token and pledge of our constant faith and abiding love.

Each of you, by the giving and receiving of these rings, and by your words, do now and forever seal these marriage vows.

Number Four:

Dick, would you now seal your vows with the gift of a ring? (Answer: "I will!") Please repeat after me as you place this ring on your bride's finger: I receive you Jane, as my wife, and I give to you this ring of gold, symbolizing the purity and endlessness of my love for you.

Jane, would you now seal your vows with the gift of a ring? (Answer: "I will!") Please repeat after me as you place this ring on your groom's finger: I receive you Dick, as my husband, and I give to you this ring of gold, symbolizing the purity and endlessness of my love for you.

Each of you, by the giving and receiving of these rings, and by your words, do now and forever seal these marriage vows.

Special Ceremonies

Couple's Communion

As I've told you, I believe you're married right now. Having made your promises, sealed with rings, everything that is marriage is in place. You have chosen for your first act as a married couple to be an act of worship as you observe the Lord's Supper.

"The Lord Jesus took bread, and when He had given thanks, He broke it and said, 'This is my body, which is for you; do this in remembrance of me.' In the same way, after supper He took the cup, saying, 'This cup is the new covenant in my blood; do this, whenever you drink it, in remembrance of me.'"[110]

(I would then serve the groom, and he would serve his bride.)

Lighting the Unity Candle

You have chosen to light a unity candle signifying the joining of your lives. The outside candles represent your two separate lives. They are two distinct lights, each capable of going its separate way. To bring joy and radiance into your home, there must be the merging of your lives just as you merge these to flames into one. From this time on, may your thoughts be for each other rather than for yourselves; may your plans be mutual; may your joys and sorrows be shared.

As you light the new candle, you will have one new flame that represents the union of your two lives into one. As this new light cannot be divided, let not your lives be divided.

---

110 First Corinthians 11:24–25

Mixing Sand

You have chosen to represent the joining of your lives by creating a piece of art as you mix these different colors of sand into one. The different colors represent your two separate lives to this moment, two distinct lives, each capable of going separate ways. To bring joy and life into your home, you must merge your lives just as you merge these colors. From this time onward may your thoughts be for each other rather than for yourselves. May your plans be mutual and may your joys and sorrows be shared.

As you mix the colors you create a piece of art. It will change over time as the natural vibrations of the earth cause the grains of sand to mix even more. As the individual grains, for all practical purposes, can never be separated, may your lives never be separated.

(When there are children who are brought into the marriage, commonly the couple will pour sand in first, creating a base, then they all together complete pouring sand.)

List of Wedding Photos

Before the ceremony:

Desired / Taken

___	___ Wedding gown on a bed with accessories
___	___ Bride at a mirror in wedding gown
___	___ Bride and mother at a mirror putting on veil
___	___ Bride and maid of honor putting on veil
___	___ Bride and sister(s) at a mirror
___	___ Each attendant holding flowers
___	___ ¾ portrait of bride
___	___ Close up portrait of bride
___	___ Bride with each attendant ¾ pose
___	___ Bride with brother(s)
___	___ Bride with sister(s)
___	___ Maid of honor putting on garter
___	___ Bride with all attendants
___	___ Bride in contemplation with bouquet
___	___ Bride at window with flower girl
___	___ Bride at window with mother
___	___ Bride with mother
___	___ Bride pinning mother's corsage
___	___ Mother kissing bride on cheek
___	___ Bride with father
___	___ Bride pinning father's boutonniere
___	___ Father kissing bride on cheek

Desired / Taken

___	___	Bride adjusting father's tie
___	___	Bride with parents
___	___	Bride sitting on father's knee
___	___	Bride coming down stairs at house
___	___	Flower girl with bride
___	___	Flower girl kissing bride on cheek
___	___	Flower girl presenting bride with flowers
___	___	Ring bearer and flower girl with bride
___	___	Ring bearer with bride
___	___	Flower girl in formal pose
___	___	Ring bearer in formal pose
___	___	Groom with mother
___	___	Mother kissing groom on cheek
___	___	Groom with father shaking hands
___	___	Groom with parents
___	___	Groom's parents
___	___	Groom in formal pose
___	___	Groom with best man
___	___	Groom with each groomsman
___	___	Groom with all groomsmen
___	___	Groom and flower girl
___	___	Groom and ring bearer
___	___	Groom with ring bearer and flower girl
___	___	Exterior of church
___	___	Marquee (if available)

During the ceremony

Desired / Taken

___	___ Groom's mother escorted down the aisle
___	___ Bride's mother escorted down the aisle
___	___ Each attendant coming down the aisle
___	___ Flower girl coming down the aisle
___	___ Ring bearer coming down the aisle
___	___ Bride and father coming down the aisle
___	___ Father kissing bride at front of aisle
___	___ Bride's father shaking hands with groom
___	___ Groom and bride presenting flowers to parents
___	___ Groom escorting bride to altar
___	___ Wedding kiss
___	___ Couple leaving altar
___	___ Bride and groom kiss in foyer
___	___ Receiving line

Photos posed after the ceremony

Desired / Taken

___	___	Couple with minister exchanging vows
___	___	Couple with minister exchanging rings
___	___	Couple signing license
___	___	Bride and groom – full length
___	___	Bride and groom ¾ poses
___	___	Bride and groom close up
___	___	Couple with best man and maid of honor
___	___	Couple with each bridesmaid and her groomsman
___	___	Couple with ring bearer and flower girl
___	___	Couple with ushers
___	___	Couple with entire wedding party
___	___	Couple with bride's parents
___	___	Couple with bride's brother(s) and sister(s)
___	___	Couple with bride's family
___	___	Couple with bride's grandparents
___	___	Couple with bride's and groom's parents
___	___	Couple with groom's parents
___	___	Couple with groom's brother(s) and sister(s)
___	___	Couple with groom's family
___	___	Couple with groom's grandparents
___	___	Couple with minister
___	___	Bride with both fathers
___	___	Bride with both mothers
___	___	Groom with both fathers
___	___	Groom with both mothers

Desired / Taken

___   ___ Bride with her parents

___   ___ Groom with his parents

___   ___ Bride with all attendants

___   ___ Bride with all bridesmaids

___   ___ Bride with all groomsmen

___   ___ Groom with all attendants

___   ___ Groom with all bridesmaids

___   ___ Groom with all groomsmen

___   ___ Musicians and singers

___   ___ Bride with special friends

___   ___ Groom with special friends

___   ___ Generation portrait (Grandmother, mother, bride)

___   ___ Generation portrait (Grandfather, father, groom)

___   ___ Couple silhouette in church door

___   ___ Couple in church door waving to friends

___   ___ Couple leaving church

___   ___ Couple through window of car

At the reception

Desired / Taken

___	___	Guests signing register
___	___	Couple entering
___	___	Couple having first dance
___	___	Bride's parents dancing
___	___	Groom's parents dancing
___	___	Bride dancing with her father
___	___	Groom dancing with his mother
___	___	Bride dancing with groom's father
___	___	Groom dancing with bride's mother
___	___	Best man proposing toast
___	___	Photo of cake
___	___	Photo of buffet table
___	___	Cutting the cake
___	___	Bride feeding cake to groom
___	___	Groom feeding cake to bride
___	___	Couple kissing over cake
___	___	Candid photos of guests
___	___	Bride throwing bouquet
___	___	Groom removing garter
___	___	Groom throwing garter
___	___	Removing the veil
___	___	Groom carrying bride through door

Appendix K
Baby Dedication Ceremony

A Baby Dedication is a ceremony in which believing parents make a commitment before the Lord to submit a child to God's will and to raise that child according to God's Word and God's ways.

Christian parents who dedicate a child are making a promise to Jesus to do everything within their power to raise their child in a godly way, until he or she can make a decision on his or her own to follow Christ.

The Bible says that children are a reward from the Lord.[111] As believers we are called to recognize that children belong first and foremost to God. In His goodness God gives children as gifts to parents. You not only have the awesome responsibility of caring for this gift, but also the wonderful privilege of enjoying the gift. Because children belong to God and are given by grace as gifts to parents, it is only proper and appropriate that children be dedicated back to God.

As you love and honor God, and as you love one another and your child, you will model before him/her a wonderful love for God that he/she will want for him/herself.

To the parents: Do you commit, by God's help and in partnership with the church, to provide him/her a Christian home of love and peace, to raise him/her in the truth of our Lord's instructions and discipline, and to encourage him/her to one day trust Jesus Christ as his Savior and Lord?

To the family: Parents have first responsibility, but parents need help and support of extended family and of the church. So I direct

---

111 Psalm 127:3

my question now to the family. Do you commit, by God's help, to be faithful in your role as family, to help and support Garret and Theresa as they raise Brayden in the ways of God?

To the congregation: And now I ask the congregation of Agape Christian Church, as members of the body of Christ, will you be faithful in your calling, to help these parents in their faithfulness to God, helping them teach and train their child in the ways of the Lord so that h/she might one day trust Him as Savior and Lord.

May God bless these parents and families, and this church as this child is dedicated to the Father, Son, and Holy Spirit.

(We also created a certificate for the parents that they can frame and mount as a reminder of their commitment made this day.)

Appendix L
Ordination Ceremonies

Elder:

In accordance with the Constitution and By–Laws of Agape Christian Church, Garrett Cadwell has been elected by the congregation to serve as Elder. It was the consensus of the people of Agape Christian Church that Garrett fits the description of Elder as set forth in First Timothy 3:1–7, Titus 1:6–9, and First Peter 5:1–4. Therefore we will at this time, formally ordain Garrett Cadwell to the office of Elder at Agape Christian Church.

To the new Elder: Garrett, in the knowledge of all the demands that shall be made upon you, and in keeping with the high standards of Christ for those who lead His people and proclaim His Gospel, do you desire to serve in the ministry of Elder of this church?

Will you affirm the following:

- Your faith in Jesus Christ as Lord and Savior, the Son of God
- Your loyalty to Him and to this church over which the Holy Spirit has called you to serve
- Your trust in the Bible as the inspired Word of God?

Garrett Cadwell, as you humbly stand before God and this congregation, receive the blessing of this church to encourage and support you in ministry as you watch over this church.

We now declare Garrett Cadwell to be ordained to the office and ministry of Elder at Agape Christian Church, duly authorized to perform all the functions pertaining to this office, and on behalf of this church, we extend to you the right hand of fellowship in recognition of your calling.

Deacon:

In accordance with the Constitution and By–Laws of Agape Christian Church, Tom Powers has been elected by the congregation to serve as Deacon. It was the consensus of the people of Agape Christian Church that Tom fits the description of Deacon as set forth in First Timothy 3:8–12. Therefore we will at this time, formally ordain Tom Powers to the office of Deacon at Agape Christian Church.

To the new Deacon: Tom Powers, have you prayerfully considered the responsibilities and obligations which the office you are about to fill carries? Will you always, seeking God's help, faithfully perform the duties of the office, endeavoring to learn and do the things that will make for the peace, purity, unity, and spiritual growth of the congregation you are called to serve?

For as much as you have been chosen by Agape Christian Church, and have declared your willingness to accept the office of Deacon, you are now, with earnest prayer for God's blessing formally ordained and declared to be Deacon of this church.

Minister/Missionary Professional:

Example One:

Read Matthew 25:31–40

In accordance with the practices and belief of Agape Christian Church, it is the prerogative and responsibility of the Elders and the congregation, under the guidance of God's Holy Spirit, to set aside certain individuals for ministry. George Bond has expressed a great desire and has demonstrated a true calling to preach the Gospel of Christ and serve as a local church minister. It is the consensus of the Elders of Agape Christian Church that Bill Grafton has been called by God for this ministry.

It is the belief of the Elders of Agape Christian Church that Bill exhibits the very love of Christ for His church. Therefore, we do set apart Bill to serve as Preaching Minister and we recommend him to other Christian congregations to avail of his service.

To the new Minister: Bill Grafton, have you prayerfully considered the responsibilities and obligations which this calling carries, and do you, with a just appreciation of the responsibilities and obligations, accept the calling?

Will you commit yourself, always seeking God's help, to faithfully perform the duties of the calling, studiously endeavoring to learn and to do the things that will bring Christ to whatever congregation in which God places you to serve?

Will you work toward the spiritual growth of such congregation that the people thereof might come to serve Christ and honor Him with their lives?

For as much as you have been examined by the Elders of Agape Christian Church, and have been found to be of outstanding character and love directed toward the people of God, and have declared your willingness and desire to accept this calling, and have committed to faithfully perform its duties, you are now, with earnest prayer for God's blessing, formally ordained and declared to be a Minister of the Gospel of Christ, with the full support and trust of Agape Christian Church.

Example Two:

Read Ephesians 4:11–12

In accordance with the laws of the State of Indiana and after consideration by the Elders of Agape Christian Church, it was agreed that Patrick Pence should be officially ordained to serve as a Minister of the Gospel with all of the associated responsibilities and authority.

It was the consensus of the Elders of Agape Christian Church that Patrick has been gifted and called to this ministry. Therefore we will at this time, formally ordain Patrick as a Minister.

Affirmation of faith.

To the new Minister: As your brother and friend, I ask you these questions to be answered from the integrity of your heart.

In the knowledge of all the demands that shall be made upon you, and in keeping with the high standards of Christ for those who lead His people and proclaim His Gospel, do you desire to serve in full–time ministry?

Do you affirm your faith in Jesus Christ as Lord and Savior, the Son of God? And do you affirm your loyalty to Him and submit your love and service to Him?

Do you affirm your trust in God's hand in your life and the empowerment and gifts of His Holy Spirit to enable you to carry out the ministry to which you are called?

Do you affirm your trust in the Bible as the inspired Word of God, and your faith in the Gospel of Christ as the power of God for salvation?

Do you declare that you will be diligent in the study of Scripture, prayerfully in your attitude toward God, and gentle, patient, and faithful in your ministry to the people of God's church?

Statement of Ordination. Patrick Pence, as you humbly stand before God and the congregation, receive the blessing of the church to encourage and support you in ministry and to watch over you in faith.

We now declare Patrick Pence to be ordained to ministry, duly authorized to perform all the functions pertaining to ministry. On behalf of this church and in accordance with the pattern of the church in the New Testament, we now place our hands on you in recognition of that fact.

Prayer

(Following each of these brief ceremonies, the Elders of Agape Christian Church placed hands on the candidate and prayed over him.)

(We also created a certificate of ordination, printed on appropriate paper, and using a more formal looking font.)

Certificate of Ordination

Be it known that

Garrett Caldwell

well known to Agape Christian Church, has, on this day February 22, 2015 been set apart to Christian service as a Elder and is hereby commended to the congregation of Agape Christian Church.

In witness thereof, we the undersigned Elders of Agape Christian Church of La Porte, Indiana do set our hand.

_____   _____

_____   _____

_____

Senior Minister

Bibliography

Brokaw, Tom, *The Greatest Generation*. Random House, 1998.

Campbell, Ross, *How to Really Love Your Child*. David C. Cook, 2015.

Chapman, Gary, *The Five Love Languages*. Northfield, 2015.

Covey, Stephen R., *The 7 Habits of Highly Effective Families*. Thriftbooks, 1997.

Gregory, John Milton, *The Seven Laws of Teaching*. Canon Press, 1886, Reprint Edition 2014.

Haugk, Kenneth, *Journey Through Grief*. Stephen Ministries, 2013.

Hayes, Ed, *A Pair of Parables*, Thomas Turkle, 2022.

Littauer, Florence, *Personality Plus*. Revell, 1983.

MacDonald, Gordon, *Building Below the Waterline*. Hendrickson Publishing, 2011.

MacDonald, Gordon, *Ordering Your Private World*. Thomas Nelson Publishing, 2007.

Romesha, Clinton, *Red Platoon*. Penguin Random House, 2016.

Sagan, Carl, *Cosmos*. Penguin Random House, 1980.

Swihart, Judson, *How Do You Say, "I Love You?"*. InterVarsity Press, 1997.

Wangerin, Walt, *As for Me and My House*. Thomas Nelson, 1987.

About the Author

Dr. Rod Nielsen

A native of Fond du Lac, Wisconsin, Dr. Rod Nielsen enrolled at Minnesota Bible College in 1972, earning his BA in Preaching Ministry in 1976. Upon graduation and feeling a call to further his studies, Rod, along with his wife Lisa, moved to Lincoln, IL to attend Lincoln Christian Seminary where he graduated in 1981 with his MA in New Testament.

In January of 1981 Rod moved to La Porte, Indiana to serve as Preaching Minister at Maple City Christian Church, a small church of about 60 people. Five years later, in 1986, Maple City Christian Church merged with a small sister church, Agape Christian Church. Early in his career, Dr. Nielsen was awarded Outstanding Young Minister by Standard Publishing. He has served on the Continuation Committee for the North American Christian Convention, co-created and led an annual growth conference for La Porte county churches, served as Chaplain to the La Porte City Police Department, and served on numerous community boards. Upon his retirement, Dr. Nielsen was awarded the Christian Servants Award from Lincoln Christian University.

In 2000 Rod pursued a Doctor of Ministry degree at Grace Theological Seminary in Winona Lake, Indiana, graduating in 2004. Because of his great love for small churches and the pastors who serve them, Dr. Nielsen chose to research and write his dissertation about how pastors of small churches can find Biblical contentment.

Following his retirement in May, 2020, Dr. Nielsen felt called to write this book from the notes of his teaching of interns and other men and women whom he had mentored during his 39 years as a pastor. He realized that few pastors have been taught these skills and concepts, yet their churches expect them to know how to carry them out. By putting these thoughts in print, Rod hopes to help both experienced and inexperienced pastors to successfully serve their congregations.

Made in the USA
Columbia, SC
28 February 2023

13007493R00133